SESAME

B is for baking

50 yummy dishes to make together

WILEY

John Wiley & Sons, Inc.

This book is dedicated to Molly, who brought Elmo and the gang into my life and changed it for the better, forever.

Special thanks go to our extremely talented panel of young recipe testers and tasters: Molly McQuillan, Danielle Tull, Simone Robbennolt, Sabrina Xuereb, Starr Silver, Sydney Caputo, Tess Brennan, Talia Crawford, and Ruby Serafin. You guys are the best!

—SUSAN McQUILLAN

Contributing Writer and Editor   Leslie A. Kimmelman

Sesame Workshop
Senior Vice President,
Worldwide Media Distribution   Scott Chambers
Vice President, Worldwide Publishing Jennifer A. Perry
Health & Education Consultant   Jane Park Woo

John Wiley & Sons
Publisher   Natalie Chapman
Senior Editor   Linda Ingroia
Production Director   Diana Cisek
Production Editor   Abby Saul
Manufacturing Manager   Kevin Watt

Interior Designer   Jowill Woodman
Photographer   Lucy Schaeffer
Food Stylist   Simon Andrews

Library of Congress Cataloging-in-Publication Data
McQuillan, Susan, 1953-
  B is for baking : 50 yummy dishes to make together / Susan McQuillan ; photographs by Lucy Schaeffer.
     p. cm.
  Includes bibliographical references and index.
  ISBN 978-0-470-63886-6 (cloth : alk. paper) 1. Baking. 2. Cookbooks. I. Schaeffer, Lucy. II. Title.
  TX763.M43 2011
  641.8'15--dc22
                              2010042337

Printed in China

10 9 8 7 6 5 4 3 2 1

There are Twiddlebugs of many colors in this book. Can you count how many? (Don't count me.) The answer is on page 128.

contents

page 108

page 64

page 14

introduction

This book contains 50 simple, wholesome recipes for great baked goods to prepare with young children and eat for breakfast, lunch, brunch, dinner, and, of course, dessert. Every recipe is marked with steps suitable for a young child to perform with or without the help of an adult. Some children will be able to perform many of these steps on their own; others may need assistance.

In addition to following specially marked steps, most children can help collect, count, sort, and measure ingredients as well as prepare some foods as indicated on the ingredient list. See the Kids in the Kitchen section (page 5) for general suggestions on what young children can do at different ages. Of course, you know your child best, and you should decide what types of ingredients and kitchen tools your child is capable of handling. At the very least, an adult should always be present when children are working in the kitchen.

For both desserts and savory dishes, healthy baking means using only as much sugar, salt, and fat as necessary. Young children quickly develop preferences for foods in terms of their flavor, texture, richness, sweetness, saltiness, and spiciness. When you bake with children, you are not only demonstrating and teaching techniques, you are helping to shape these preferences. You can also point out the number of servings and serving size in the recipes they help prepare. Serving sizes are generally standard and demonstrate appropriate portion size—how much of a particular food to eat.

The recipe ingredients in *B is for Baking* strike a balance between all-purpose white flour and more wholesome options such as whole-wheat flour, oatmeal, cornmeal, and wheat germ. (For information on wheat-free baking, see Ingredient Substitutions, page 10.) In most cases, the recipes call for olive oil or vegetable oil as healthier alternatives to some or all of the butter that would normally be used. In each recipe, there's just enough sugar and salt to ensure successful baking and a satisfying end result. Most importantly, almost all of these recipes are baked or served with fruits and vegetables or other wholesome ingredients.

KIDS IN THE KITCHEN

every recipe in this cookbook highlights at least one task that a young child can perform. Choose recipes with steps that you think your own child can accomplish. The age-appropriate list of tasks provided below is adapted from The National Network for Child Care's recommendations for cooking with children. The best advice, however, is to trust your own instincts: if a task seems too difficult for your child, don't frustrate him by making him do it. Invite him to help in another way. Remember that even a very young child can help by handing you an ingredient or a small utensil, such as a wooden spoon.

Children of different ages exhibit varying degrees of skill in the kitchen, but for the most part, **the average two-year-old can help:**

- wash and scrub fruits and vegetables;
- wipe off the work surface;
- carry utensils and small equipment to the work surface;
- crush crackers and cookies into crumbs;
- tear up lettuce and spinach leaves;
- dip one ingredient into another;
- arrange foods on baking sheets and trays;

and an average three-year-old can do whatever a two-year-old can do, plus help:

- cut soft foods with a plastic serrated knife;
- pour measured liquid ingredients into a bowl of dry ingredients;
- stir or whisk ingredients together;
- mix batter;

while an average four- and five-year-old can do all of the above, plus help:

- measure dry ingredients;
- mash soft foods together;
- peel a banana or an orange if the skin has been loosened for them;
- crack an egg into a bowl (but have some extra eggs on hand!);
- set and clear the table.

Slightly older siblings and friends can help plan the meal, read the recipe out loud, supervise younger cooks, and take on some of the more complicated cooking tasks such as juicing lemons, leveling off dry ingredients, and measuring liquid ingredients.

> **Remember:** Children must be supervised in the kitchen at all times, even when performing age-appropriate tasks.

safe Baking

It goes without saying that children should never go near a hot stove or oven, or any sharp objects. But it's easy to forget even basic kitchen safety rules when you're busy cooking and baking. Children should also know how to stay safe in the kitchen, so here is a read-aloud review of the rules from the Sesame Street gang.

Kitchen Safety Tips

- **There should ALWAYS be a grown-up** in the kitchen to supervise all food preparation, cooking, and cleaning up.

- **Always ask a grown-up for** help when you can't reach something or don't know how to do something.

- **Always wash your hands** before you touch food. Also wash your hands after you touch any type of meat, poultry, or fish, before you touch anything else. If you have to sneeze or cough or wipe your nose, remember to wash your hands afterward, before you touch the food again. Remember to keep your fingers and hands away from your face and mouth while you are preparing food.

- **Roll up long sleeves; tie back long hair.**

- **Set up your own separate workspace for** preparing food, away from the oven and from any hot or sharp kitchen utensils.

- **Take your time and do only one thing at a** time. There's no hurry!

- **Never touch kitchen knives, food** processor or blender blades, graters or peelers, or any other sharp object in the kitchen. Ask a grown-up to show you how to use a plastic knife to help slice soft foods, by cutting away from your fingers so you don't get hurt.

- **Never go near a hot stove or** oven. It is a grown-up's job to cook with pots and pans on top of the stove and put food in the oven and take it back out again.

- **Clean up leftover food and** used equipment right away so your workspace stays organized and safe.

- **Tell a grown-up immediately if you see** the handle of a pot sticking out from the top of the stove, or wires hanging off a counter, or sharp items lying around the kitchen.

Better Baking: Tips and Techniques

One of the most important rules to teach your child about cooking and baking, after basic safety, is to read a recipe through from beginning to end before you begin to gather ingredients and equipment. Prepare and measure all ingredients before you start mixing ingredients together. By the time you begin following the recipe directions, the ingredients should be prepped, lined up, and ready to go. In addition to being the most efficient way to cook, being well prepared also helps ensure safety. Here are some other basic baking tips:

- Always preheat the oven for at least 10 minutes.

- Use the correct pan size. The correct size can be a different pan than what is called for in the recipe, as long as it is the same volume. (See Pan Substitutions, page 10.)

- If an ingredient such as an egg is supposed to be at room temperature, take it out of the refrigerator 30 minutes before using.

- Mix ingredients together as indicated in the directions for each recipe unless you're truly comfortable knowing how to adjust the time and alternative techniques needed. The way you mix—for instance, by hand or with an electric mixer—can affect the final result.

- Remember: The best-tasting dishes are made with the freshest, best-quality ingredients.

Baking how-to's

To measure dry ingredients: Use metal or plastic nested dry measuring cups. Lightly spoon flour and other dry ingredients into dry cup measuring cups, and level off the top with the edge of a spatula. Do not dip the measuring cup into a bag of flour. With measuring spoons, dip the spoon into the ingredient (such as baking powder, baking soda, salt, herb, or spice) and level off with a spatula. You can also spoon or pour an ingredient into a measuring spoon and level off, if that method makes more sense, such as when the measuring spoon doesn't fit into the ingredient container.

To measure liquid ingredients: Use glass or plastic liquid measuring cups. Place the liquid measuring cup on a flat, level surface such as a kitchen counter. Pour the ingredient right up to the line indicated for the measured amount.

To separate an egg: Young children will do best using an egg separator, which is available in any baking supply store or the cookware section of most department stores. Have the child hold the separator over a bowl while an adult or an older child cracks the egg and drops it into the separator. The yolk will remain in the separator and the egg white will fall into the bowl. A child can then transfer the yolk to

another bowl. To separate an egg by hand, tap the egg gently on the counter to crack slightly, and hold it over a bowl. Split the shell open, tilt the egg slightly so that only the egg white falls into the bowl. The yolk tends to stay in the bottom of one half of the shell. Transfer the yolk from one half of the shell to the other and, at the same time, allow the remaining egg white to fall into the bowl. Alternatively, pour the remaining egg into your hand, cradling the yolk in your palm and letting the white drip through your fingers and into the bowl. Drop the yolk into a separate bowl or container. Be sure to wash hands after separating eggs and before proceeding with recipe.

To beat egg whites: When you beat egg whites, you are whipping air into the mixture to achieve volume. You will get the most volume from eggs that are at room temperature. Always use completely clean bowls and beaters or the eggs will not beat properly. With the mixer set on medium-low to medium, it takes about half a minute to beat egg whites to the "frothy" stage, which creates a layer of bubbles on top. Continue with the mixer on medium to medium-high. You have reached the "soft peak" stage when the egg whites are creamy and opaque, with a rippled surface. When you turn off your electric mixer and lift your beaters, the egg white peaks that form will fold right back down into the mixture. With several more seconds or perhaps a minute of beating, you will reach the "hard peak" stage, which is when you lift the beaters and the peaks that form remain upright.

To cut butter into flour: Children can use a pastry blender. Alternatively, adults can use two knives to cut butter into flour until the mixture resembles coarse crumbs.

To fold ingredients: When a recipe instructs you to fold one mixture into another, use a rubber spatula to gently incorporate the ingredients with a slow, wide stirring motion, until just blended. Do not overmix.

> **Tip:** It is a good idea to test often for peak stages once the egg white mixture is opaque, because beaten whites can quickly go from soft peak (the peak flops over) to firm, or hard peak (the peak is stiff) to over-beaten.

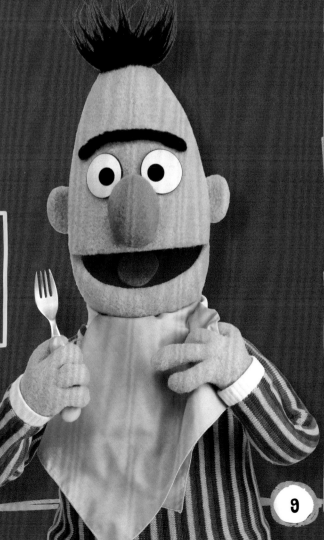

pan substitutions

If you don't have the pan called for in any recipe, you can usually substitute another pan, and it doesn't necessarily have to be the same size or shape. What's most important is that the capacity, or volume, is the same and that you keep an eye on how the food is cooking, to make sure you've adjusted the cooking time properly. Also keep in mind:

- If you are substituting a shallower pan than what is called for in the recipe, reduce the baking time by about one-fourth. For example, if the baking time in the recipe is 1 hour, bake in a shallower pan for 45 minutes.

- If you are substituting a deeper pan than what is called for in the recipe, increase the baking time by about one-fourth. For example, if the original baking time is 35 to 40 minutes, add another 10 minutes for a range of 45 to 50 minutes.

- With the exception of pie plates, recipes are written for metal baking pans. If you are substituting a glass pan for a metal pan, reduce the oven temperature by 25°F. For pie plates, the temperature remains the same for glass or metal.

ingredient substitutions

The recipes in this book were developed and tested using the ingredients listed. Substitutions are often possible, however, if you don't have all the listed ingredients on hand, to accommodate a food allergy or sensitivity, or because your family simply prefers something different. Dairy ingredients in particular lend themselves to a variety of substitutions and alternatives.

Common Baking Pan Substitutes:

1-quart (or 4-cup) baking dish	8-inch round layer cake pan or 9-inch pie plate
1½-quart (or 6-cup) baking dish	8 or 9-inch round layer cake pan or 10-inch pie plate
2-quart (or 8-cup) baking dish	8x8x2-inch square pan or 11x7x1½-inch baking dish
Two 9-inch-round layer cake pans	Two 8x8x2-inch square cake pans or 13x9x2-inch baking pan
9x5x3-inch loaf pan	9x9x2-inch square cake pan
9-inch angel cake tube pan	10 x 3¾-inch Bundt pan
10x4-inch angel cake or tube pan	18 cups
9x3½-inch angel cake or tube pan	12 cups
9 x 3½-inch tube or Bundt pan	9 cups

Elmo likes to dish about dishes!

Soy milk, rice milk, almond milk, and light coconut milk can be substituted for cow's milk in most baked goods. Other dairy alternatives, such as soy- and rice-based cheeses and yogurts, can also be used in place of conventional products, though the final result is likely to have a different flavor or texture than the original.

Greek yogurt is similar to strained yogurt. To make your own Greek-style yogurt, line a strainer with several layers of cheesecloth. Place the strainer over a bowl. Spoon regular yogurt into the lined strainer and place the strainer and bowl in the refrigerator for at least several hours to drain. Discard the liquid (whey) in the bowl and use the drained yogurt in place of Greek yogurt in any recipe.

If a recipe calls for buttermilk and you don't have any on hand, for each cup of buttermilk called for in the recipe, you can substitute 1 tablespoon vinegar mixed with enough milk to make 1 cup, or ¾ cup yogurt mixed with ¼ cup milk.

Substituting different types of flour for wheat flours (all-purpose, bread, and whole-wheat flours) in standard baking recipes is tricky but it is often possible. Wheat flour provides baked goods with the structure and texture most people have come to expect. Gluten-free baked goods, made with non-wheat flours (such as soy flour, tapioca flour, rice flour, and potato starch), usually incorporate gluten substitutes to re-create the structure and texture of wheat products. These gluten substitutes, available in most health food stores, include xanthum gum, guar gum and pre-gel starch. The standard formula is 1 teaspoon of gluten substitute for each cup of gluten-free flour used. However, you will probably want to experiment with different flour blends and different gluten substitutes to find mixtures that work best for you.

A note about food allergies: When you are cooking with other people's children, always double check with parents or guardians about possible food allergies. Common allergens include peanuts and other nuts, fish, shellfish, eggs, milk and other dairy products, soy, and wheat. If allergies exist, be sure to carefully read the ingredient list on all food labels to avoid the offending food. Even if a product does not contain an allergen, it may have been processed on equipment that also processes common allergens. This information is normally printed just below the ingredient list on the food label. When a child has food allergies, he or she should not even be in the same room with any product that contains the allergen, because food particles can become airborne and be inhaled.

A note about young children and choking: Young children are still learning to chew and swallow properly, as their teeth continue to develop and they learn how to eat different types of food. All firm foods, such as many raw fruits and vegetables, dried fruit and other sticky foods, and nuts and other very hard foods, must be cut into small pieces or finely chopped or ground so they are safe for children to swallow.

Breakfast Bake-off

When it comes to getting a great start to the day, you can't beat a home-baked breakfast. Family favorites such as muffins, French toast, and oven pancakes all taste better—and are better for you—when you make them yourself.

Several university studies have suggested that people who eat breakfast develop healthier eating habits in general and are less likely to overeat later in the day than those who don't. At school, children who eat breakfast have more energy and perform better in the classroom and on tests.

Of course, breakfast is just one part of an overall healthy diet that includes a variety of foods from all the food groups and emphasizes plenty of fresh fruits and vegetables, whole grains, and lean proteins.

You may not have time to bake breakfast from scratch every day, but when you do, you'll appreciate having these simple, wholesome ideas on hand.

Tip: You can use fresh bread, but French toast is a great way to use up leftover or day-old bread, too. In fact, slightly stale bread may hold up a little better and retain more of its texture than fresh. If you like, you can leave sliced fresh bread out at room temperature, uncovered, for an hour or two before assembling this dish.

Big Bird's Favorite Peachy Baked French Toast

Preparation time: 10 minutes • Baking time: 30 minutes • Makes 6 servings (6 slices)

Fresh peaches are best if they're in season and they're ripe and sweet. Otherwise, frozen sliced peaches will do just fine.

ingredients

- **6 thick slices challah bread, brioche, or French bread**
- **3 large eggs**
- **1 cup low-fat milk**
- **1 tablespoon sugar**
- **¼ teaspoon ground cinnamon**
- **⅛ teaspoon ground nutmeg**
- **Pinch of salt**
- **2 peaches, thinly sliced (or 2 cups sliced frozen peaches, thawed)**
- **1 tablespoon orange juice**
- **1 tablespoon real maple syrup**
- **Fresh raspberries (optional)**

equipment

- **Baking dish (11×7 inches)**
- **Medium bowls (2)**
- **Whisk or forks (2)**
- **Measuring cups**
- **Measuring spoons**
- **Cooling rack**
- **Wide spatula**

1 Lightly grease an 11x7-inch baking dish.

2 Line the dish with bread slices in a single layer.

3 In a medium bowl, with a whisk or fork, lightly beat the eggs until just blended. Stir in the milk, sugar, cinnamon, nutmeg, and salt. Pour evenly over bread in dish. Let stand 10 minutes while preheating the oven.

4 Preheat the oven to 350°F. In another medium bowl, with a clean fork, toss together the peaches, orange juice, and syrup. Turn bread slices over. Scatter the peaches evenly over the bread.

5 Bake 25 to 30 minutes or until golden. Transfer to cooling rack and let stand 15 minutes before serving. Use a wide spatula to transfer individual squares of toast to plates. Garnish with raspberries, if you like.

Peaches were first grown in China. Some people there believed that eating peaches assured you of living a long life.

Tip: If you don't have a skillet with an ovenproof handle, you can bake this pancake in a deep-dish pie plate.

grover's german pancake

Preparation time: 10 minutes • Baking time: 25 minutes • Makes one 10-inch pancake; 4 to 6 servings

You can top a German pancake with any type of cut-up fruit or berries. Like all pancakes, it's great with real maple syrup, too!

ingredients

- 1 tablespoon butter
- 1 tablespoon olive oil
- 6 large eggs
- 1 cup low-fat milk
- ½ teaspoon pure vanilla extract
- 1 cup all-purpose flour
- ¼ cup toasted wheat germ
- ¼ teaspoon salt
- 2 cups mixed sliced bananas and strawberries
- Confectioner's sugar (optional)

equipment

- **Ovenproof skillet (10-inch)**
- **Large bowl**
- **Whisk or fork**
- **Measuring spoons**
- **Measuring cups**
- **Heatproof pot holder**
- **Cooling rack**
- **Knife for slicing fruit**

1 Preheat oven to 450°F. Place butter and oil in a large (10-inch), heavy, ovenproof skillet. Place the skillet in the oven while it preheats. Meanwhile, prepare pancake batter.

2 **Kids!** In a large bowl, using a whisk or fork, briskly stir the eggs until light and frothy. Add the milk, vanilla, flour, wheat germ, and salt. Keep stirring, gently now, until the batter is well-blended.

3 When the oven is preheated, use a heatproof pot holder to quickly tilt the skillet by the handle and swirl the butter and oil around to coat it.

4 Pour the batter into the hot skillet.

5 Bake 20 to 25 minutes or until very puffy and golden brown around the edge. Transfer the skillet to a rack to cool 1 minute. (Pancake will deflate as it cools.) Cut 4 to 6 individual wedges from the skillet, or transfer the entire pancake to a serving plate. Top with bananas and strawberries, dust lightly with confectioner's sugar, if using, and serve.

> There are pancake-like foods all around the world: in France, they have crêpes; in Russia, blinis; in the U.S., some people call them flapjacks.

Tip: If you don't have ripe, sweet strawberries in season, skip the berries and use strawberry jam to make Strawberry Surprise Muffins instead: Fill the muffin cups one-third of the way full, top with a small spoonful of jam, then fill the cup two-thirds of the way full with more batter. Bake as directed.

Abby Cadabby's Disappearing Strawberry Muffins

Preparation time: 15 minutes • Baking time: 25 minutes • Makes 12 muffins

These muffins are so yummy, they disappear in minutes! Try them with chopped fresh peaches, nectarines, or other berries in season.

Ingredients

- 1 cup all-purpose flour
- ½ cup whole-wheat flour
- ⅓ cup sugar
- ¼ cup cornmeal
- 1 teaspoon baking powder
- ½ teaspoon baking soda
- ¼ teaspoon salt
- 1 cup low-fat plain yogurt
- ⅓ cup olive oil
- 1 large egg
- 2 cups strawberries, hulled and chopped

Equipment

- Muffin pan (for 12 cups)
- Cup liners (optional)
- Medium bowl
- Whisk
- Measuring cups
- Measuring spoons
- Large bowl
- Rubber spatula
- Toothpick
- Cooling rack

1. Preheat the oven to 400°F.

2. **Kids!** Line 12 muffin cups with paper or foil liners. (Adults: If you don't have liners, lightly grease each cup.)

3. In a medium bowl, whisk together the all-purpose flour, whole-wheat flour, sugar, cornmeal, baking powder, baking soda, and salt; set aside.

4. **Kids!** In a large bowl, use a rubber spatula to stir together the yogurt and oil, then stir in the egg until well-blended. Stir in the flour mixture just until mixed. Fold in the strawberries.

5. Fill the muffin cups two-thirds of the way full.

6. Bake for 20 to 25 minutes or until a toothpick inserted in the center of one muffin comes out clean. Transfer to rack to cool for a minute or two. Turn the muffins out to cool further.

> Look at the little bumps on each strawberry. It's the only fruit that has seeds on the outside—about 200 on each berry!

Lots of animals eat blueberries, too—like birds, deer, and bears. 1 berry, 2 berries, 3 cheers for blueberries!

Tip: If you are using frozen berries, do not allow the berries to thaw. Toss them with a little flour before adding them to the batter.

ELMO'S BERRY DELICIOUS BLUEBERRY MUFFINS

Preparation time: 15 minutes • Baking time: 25 minutes • Makes 12 muffins

A subtle hint of lemon from freshly grated lemon rind gives these gems extra-special flavor.

Ingredients

- 1 cup all-purpose flour
- ¼ cup toasted wheat germ
- 1 teaspoon baking powder
- ¼ teaspoon salt
- ⅓ cup sugar
- ¼ cup (½ stick) butter
- ¼ cup olive or vegetable oil
- Grated rind of 1 lemon (1 teaspoon)
- 2 large eggs
- 1 cup fresh blueberries
- 2 tablespoons sugar, combined with ¼ teaspoon ground cinnamon

Equipment

- Muffin pan (for 12 cups)
- Cup liners (optional)
- Medium bowl
- Whisk
- Measuring cups
- Measuring spoons
- Large bowl
- Electric mixer
- Rubber spatula
- Toothpick
- Cooling rack

1 Preheat the oven to 400°F.

2 Line 12 muffin cups with paper or foil liners. (Adults: If you don't have liners, lightly grease each cup.)

3 In a medium bowl, whisk together the flour, wheat germ, baking powder, and salt; set aside.

4 In a large bowl, with an electric mixer, beat the sugar and butter until well-blended and creamy. Beat in the oil and lemon rind. Add in the eggs, one a time, beating well after each. By hand, use a rubber spatula to stir in the flour mixture just until blended. Fold in the blueberries. Fill each muffin cup about two-thirds of the way full. Sprinkle each with cinnamon-sugar mix.

5 Bake 20 to 25 minutes or until a toothpick inserted in the middle of one muffin comes out clean. Transfer to rack to cool for a minute or two. Turn the muffins out to cool further.

Tips:
- It's okay to let kids help combine the dry ingredients and wet, but remind them to keep stirring to a minimum—overbeating can result in tough muffins.

- If you are working with more than one child, and everyone wants a turn, try the "one stir apiece" approach.

Big Bird's good·for·you, good·for·me oatmeal muffins

Preparation time: 10 minutes • Baking time: 15 minutes • Makes 12 muffins

Who knew healthy eating could taste this good? Yogurt adds protein and calcium and helps to keep these muffins moist.

ingredients

- 1 cup old-fashioned rolled oats
- ½ cup firmly packed light brown sugar
- 1 cup low-fat yogurt, or buttermilk
- 1 large egg
- ½ cup olive oil
- ½ cup all-purpose flour
- ½ cup whole-wheat flour
- 1 teaspoon baking powder
- ½ teaspoon baking soda
- ½ teaspoon salt
- ½ cup finely chopped dried cherries, golden raisins, or dried cranberries, finely chopped (optional)

equipment

- Large bowls (2)
- Measuring cups
- Measuring spoons
- Rubber spatula
- Muffin pan (for 12 cups)
- Cup liners (optional)
- Whisk
- Toothpick
- Cooling rack

1 In a large bowl, with a rubber spatula, stir together the oats, brown sugar, yogurt, egg, and oil. Be careful not to overmix. Let stand 15 minutes while the oven is preheating.

2 Preheat the oven to 400°F.

3 Line 12 muffin cups with paper or foil liners. (Adults: If you don't have liners, lightly grease each cup.)

4 In another large bowl, whisk together the all-purpose flour, whole-wheat flour, baking powder, baking soda, and salt until well-mixed. Add to oat mixture, stirring with the spatula until just combined. Gently fold in cherries. Divide batter evenly among prepared muffin tins (about ⅓ cup batter per muffin).

5 Bake muffins 15 minutes or until golden on top and a toothpick inserted in the center of a muffin comes out clean. Transfer to rack to cool for a minute or two. Turn the muffins out to cool further.

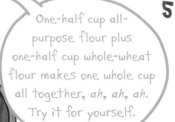

One-half cup all-purpose flour plus one-half cup whole-wheat flour makes one whole cup all together, *ah, ah, ah.* Try it for yourself.

zoe's Breakfast Jam Cake

Preparation time: 20 minutes • Baking time: 25 minutes • Makes 16 servings

This kids' version of a simple coffee cake contains whole-wheat flour, oats, yogurt, and almonds—all the makings of a wholesome, tasty breakfast. To round out the meal, serve with orange slices and a glass of milk.

Ingredients

- 1 cup all-purpose flour
- ½ cup whole-wheat flour
- 1 teaspoon baking soda
- ½ teaspoon salt
- ½ cup uncooked old-fashioned or quick-cooking oats
- ½ cup dry roasted, unsalted almonds, finely ground
- 2 tablespoons granulated sugar
- ½ cup packed light or dark brown sugar
- 2 tablespoons butter
- 2 tablespoons olive or vegetable oil
- 2 large eggs
- 1 cup low-fat plain yogurt
- 1 teaspoon vanilla extract
- ½ cup strawberry or other flavored jam, preserves, or fruit spread

Equipment

- Baking pan (8-inch-square)
- Medium bowl
- Whisk
- Rubber spatula
- Measuring cups
- Measuring spoons
- Small bowl
- Large bowl
- Electric mixer
- Wooden spoon
- Metal spoon
- Toothpick
- Cooling rack

1 Preheat the oven to 350°F. Lightly grease an 8-inch-square baking pan.

2 Kids! In a medium bowl, whisk together the all-purpose flour, whole-wheat flour, baking soda, and salt until well-mixed. Whisk in the oats.

3 Kids! In a small bowl, with a spatula, combine the ground almonds and granulated sugar.

4 In a large bowl, with an electric mixer on medium-high speed, beat together the brown sugar, butter, and oil until light and fluffy. Beat in the eggs, one at a time. Beat in the yogurt and vanilla.

5 Carefully add the flour mixture to the batter, and stir with a wooden spoon until just mixed. Spread half the batter in the oiled pan.

6 Kids! Use a spoon to drop puddles of jam all over the top of the batter. Sprinkle the batter evenly with half the almond-sugar mixture.

7 Top with remaining batter, spreading gently to cover evenly.

8 Kids! Sprinkle the remaining almond-sugar mixture evenly over the top of the cake.

9 Bake 25 minutes or until a toothpick inserted in the center comes out clean. Transfer to cooling rack for at least 20 minutes before cutting and serving. Cut into 16 small squares.

Tips:
• For very small children, be sure to grind the nuts very finely before adding them to the cake.

• For more almond flavor, add ¼ teaspoon almond extract along with the vanilla.

This jam cake makes me feel like dancing in my jammies!

Bert's veggie sleepover strata

Preparation time: 20 minutes plus resting time • Resting time: 4 hours or overnight
Baking time: 40 minutes • Makes 6 servings

This savory, prepare-ahead dish is a cross between a quiche and a bread pudding. It's a good recipe to have on hand if you're expecting a crowd for breakfast or brunch, or anytime you want to serve a warm, hearty meal early in the day but prefer to get it ready the night before.

Tips:

• When choosing bread for a strata, the thicker and denser the slice, the better. If possible, buy an unsliced loaf of whole-grain bread and cut it yourself into 1-inch-thick slices.

• Use any combination of cooked vegetables your family prefers; leftovers work well, too. Some combinations to consider are corn and tomato, zucchini and mushrooms, chopped broccoli and tomato, or chopped sweet red and green peppers with onion.

Ingredients

- 6 slices multi-grain bread, cut diagonally in half
- 1 teaspoon olive or vegetable oil
- 1 medium onion, finely chopped
- 2 medium zucchini, halved lengthwise and thinly sliced
- 2 plum tomatoes, cored and finely chopped
- 2 cups shredded Swiss, Monterey Jack, or Cheddar cheese, or a combination of cheeses
- 6 large eggs
- 1½ cups low-fat milk
- 1 tablespoon spicy brown or Dijon mustard

Equipment

- Baking dish (11×7 inches)
- Large skillet
- Rubber spatula
- Measuring cups
- Large bowl
- Measuring spoons
- Whisk
- Plastic wrap

1 With the help of an adult, lightly grease an 11x7-inch baking dish. Place the bread in the dish in one layer, with the slices slightly overlapping.

2 Heat the oil in a large skillet over medium heat. Add the onion and cook until tender, about 5 minutes. Add the zucchini and cook, stirring occasionally, 5 minutes longer. Remove the skillet from the heat and use a rubber spatula to stir in the tomatoes. Spread the vegetables evenly over the bread.

3 Sprinkle the tomatoes and cheese over the vegetables.

4 In a large bowl, whisk together the eggs, milk, and mustard until smooth.

5 Pour the egg mixture over the vegetables and cheese. Cover the baking dish with plastic wrap and refrigerate for at least 4 hours or overnight.

6 To bake, preheat the oven to 350°F. Bake the strata, uncovered, until the top is puffy and brown and the center is set, about 30 to 40 minutes. Remove the dish from the oven and let stand for 15 minutes before cutting and serving.

Z is for Zucchini.

Zzzz...

27

Tips:
- For added flavor, crumble a little cooked turkey bacon into the egg mixture before baking.
- You can substitute an equal amount of torn-up regular spinach leaves, kale, or Swiss chard for the baby spinach leaves.

OSCAR'S BAKED SPINACH OMELET

Preparation time: 15 minutes • Baking time: 20 minutes • Makes one 9-inch omelet; 4 to 6 servings

A baked omelet is one of the easiest ways to make eggs. While the omelet is baking, your hands are free to make toast or another side dish, and the kids can help set the table.

Ingredients

- 4 cups baby spinach leaves, washed thoroughly
- 1 tablespoon olive oil
- ¼ cup finely chopped onion
- 6 large eggs
- ¼ cup grated Parmesan cheese
- 2 tablespoons low-fat milk
- ¼ teaspoon salt
- ⅛ teaspoon pepper
- ¼ cup shredded Swiss or Cheddar cheese or crumbled feta or goat cheese

Equipment

- Pie plate (9-inch)
- Small skillet
- Medium bowl
- Whisk
- Measuring cups
- Measuring spoons

Spinach is green, like me! On your next trip to the market, see how many other green vegetables you can spot.

1 Preheat the oven to 350°F. Lightly grease a 9-inch pie plate.

 2 Remove the stems from the spinach leaves.

3 Heat the oil in a small skillet over medium heat. Add the onion and cook, stirring occasionally, for 2 minutes or until softened. Add the spinach in batches, cooking and stirring until all the leaves are wilted. Remove from heat.

 4 Meanwhile, in a medium bowl, whisk together the eggs, Parmesan cheese, milk, salt, and pepper.

5 Spread the spinach mixture over the bottom of the pie plate.

 6 With the help of an adult, pour the egg mixture over the spinach. Sprinkle shredded cheese on top.

7 Bake 20 minutes or until puffy and lightly browned on top. Cut into segments to serve.

I like to measure, don't you?

QUICK BREADS and BISCUITS

Quick breads and biscuits are a great introduction to baking because they involve little more than measuring, stirring, and mixing. It's easy for children to participate in almost every step.

Children like quick breads, or batter breads, because they are usually soft, moist, flavorful, and muffin-like in texture. Quick breads can be sweet or savory, and incorporate many healthy foods that children love, such as cheese, bananas, and shredded vegetables.

Soft, flaky biscuits can be served with any meal. Plain varieties, such as Abby Cadabby's Heavenly Biscuits, can also be used as a base for fresh fruit desserts, such as strawberry shortcake or an upside-down apple cobbler. Tomato biscuits and sweet potato biscuits show children once again how versatile vegetables can be.

Tip: Use very ripe bananas—the ones that have freckles all over their skin or have turned from yellow to brown—for the sweetest-tasting banana bread.

Oscar's Really Rotten Banana Bread

Preparation time: 15 minutes • Baking time: 1 hour • Makes 1 loaf (8 to 12 slices)

Oat bran adds fiber and smooth texture to this loaf, while raisins add sweetness.

Ingredients

- **1 cup all-purpose flour**
- **½ cup whole-wheat flour**
- **½ cup oat bran**
- **1 teaspoon baking soda**
- **½ teaspoon salt**
- **2 large or 3 medium bananas**
- **1 cup brown sugar**
- **½ cup olive oil**
- **1 egg**
- **½ cup golden or black raisins (optional)**

Equipment

- **Loaf pan (9x5x3-inch)**
- **Medium bowls (2)**
- **Whisk**
- **Measuring cups**
- **Measuring spoons**
- **Large bowl**
- **Electric mixer**
- **Wooden spoon**
- **Toothpick**
- **Cooling rack**

1 Preheat the oven to 350°F. Lightly grease a 9x5x3-inch loaf pan.

2 In a medium bowl, whisk together the all-purpose flour, whole-wheat flour, oat bran, baking soda, and salt.

3 In another medium bowl, mash the bananas with the back of a fork.

4 In a large bowl, with an electric mixer on medium, beat together the sugar, bananas, oil, and egg. Add the dry ingredients and mix until blended.

5 With a wooden spoon, stir in raisins, if using. With the help of an adult, scrape the batter into the oiled pan.

6 Bake for 1 hour or until a toothpick inserted in the center comes out clean. Transfer to rack to cool for 10 minutes. Turn the loaf out onto the rack to cool completely.

Who knew something so rotten could taste so sweet?

Tip: Although it may be tempting to eat this bread warm out of the oven, it must be cooled completely before slicing and serving.

Big Bird's Favorite Parmesan Loaf

Preparation time: 15 minutes • Baking time: 50 minutes • Makes 1 loaf (12 slices)

Big Bird sometimes likes cheese in his bread, instead of on top of it. This moist loaf goes great with soup for lunch or dinner, or even with eggs for breakfast.

Ingredients

- 1 cup all-purpose flour
- 1 teaspoon baking powder
- 1 teaspoon baking soda
- ¼ teaspoon salt
- 2 large eggs
- 1 cup low-fat plain yogurt
- 2 tablespoons mustard
- ½ cup grated Parmesan cheese
- ⅛ cup finely chopped fresh dill or 1 tablespoon dried dill (optional)

Equipment

- Loaf pan (9×5×3-inch)
- Small bowl
- Measuring cups
- Measuring spoons
- Whisk
- Medium bowl
- Toothpick
- Cooling rack

1 Preheat the oven to 350°F. Lightly grease a 9x5x3-inch loaf pan.

2 Kids! In a small bowl, whisk together the flour, baking powder, baking soda, and salt.

3 Kids! In a medium bowl, stir together the eggs, yogurt, mustard, Parmesan cheese, and dill, if using.

4 Kids! With the help of an adult, add the flour mixture to the egg mixture and stir just until combined. Pour the batter into the prepared pan.

5 Bake 50 minutes or until a toothpick inserted in the center comes out clean and the top of the loaf is golden brown. Transfer to cooling rack for 15 minutes. Turn the loaf out onto the rack to cool completely.

How smart is your nose? Close your eyes and ask a grown-up to pass foods with different smells under your nose. Try dill, onion, lemon, and Parmesan cheese, for example. Can you identify them?

Tips:
- You can vary this recipe by adding ingredients to the egg mixture as you make the batter. Try ½ cup fresh, drained, canned, or thawed frozen corn kernels, or an equal amount of sweet red or green peppers sautéed in a little olive oil.

- With any variation, you can add 1½ cups shredded Cheddar or Monterey Jack cheese, or spice it up with 1 tablespoon finely chopped jalapeño pepper.

Rosita's Skillet Cornbread

Preparation time: 15 minutes • Baking time: 25 minutes • Makes 8 servings

Serve in wedges topped with chili or another stew, or as a side dish with baked ham.

Ingredients

- 1 cup all-purpose flour
- 1 cup fine yellow cornmeal
- 2 teaspoons baking powder
- ½ teaspoon baking soda
- ½ teaspoon salt
- 2 large eggs
- 1 cup low-fat plain yogurt
- ¼ cup olive oil
- 2 tablespoons honey

Equipment

- Heavy skillet (9- or 10-inch)
- Large bowl
- Whisk
- Measuring cups
- Measuring spoons
- Small bowl
- Rubber spatula
- Toothpick
- Cooling rack

1 Preheat the oven to 375°F. Lightly grease a heavy 9- or 10-inch skillet.

 2 In a large bowl, whisk together the flour, cornmeal, sugar, baking powder, baking soda, and salt.

 3 In a small bowl, stir together the eggs, yogurt, and oil. Stir into the flour mixture just until blended. Scrape the batter into the oiled skillet.

4 Bake 20 to 25 minutes or until a toothpick inserted in the middle of the loaf comes out clean. Transfer to a rack to cool slightly before cutting into wedges and serving.

It's baked in a circle, and then— ta da!—triangles!

Cookie monster's Dee-licious zucchini Bread

Preparation time: 15 minutes • Baking time: 1 hour for bread, 25 minutes for muffins
Makes 2 loaves (8×4-inch, 12 slices each) or 24 muffins (1 loaf and 12 muffins!)

There's a little less sugar and a little more whole-grain goodness in these loaves than in classic zucchini breads, but they're still sweet and spicy, and they taste even better the next day. This batter makes great muffins, too!

Tip: This recipe freezes well, for up to several months. For easier serving from the freezer, slice the bread and wrap the individual slices in plastic or freezer wrap. Place the wrapped slices in a freezer bag or covered container, for extra protection.

ingredients

- 2 cups all-purpose flour
- 1 cup whole-wheat flour
- 1 tablespoon ground cinnamon
- ⅛ teaspoon ground nutmeg
- 1 teaspoon baking soda
- ¼ teaspoon baking powder
- 1 teaspoon salt
- 3 eggs
- 3¾ cups sugar
- 1 cup olive or vegetable oil
- 1 teaspoon vanilla extract
- 2 cups grated zucchini (2 medium zucchini)
- 1 cup drained, crushed pineapple

equipment

- Two loaf pans (9×5×3-inch) or two 12-cup muffin pans
- Large bowl
- Whisk
- Measuring cups
- Measuring spoons
- Medium bowl
- Spoon for stirring
- Rubber spatula
- Toothpick

1 Preheat the oven to 325°F. Grease and flour two 9x5x3-inch loaf pans or line 24 muffin pan cups with cupcake liners.

 2 In a large bowl, whisk together the all-purpose flour, whole-wheat flour, cinnamon, nutmeg, baking soda, baking powder, and salt until well-mixed.

 3 In a medium bowl, with a rubber spatula, stir together the eggs, sugar, oil, and vanilla. Stir in the zucchini and pineapple.

4 Stir the zucchini mixture into the flour mixture until well-mixed. Divide the batter between the loaf pans or muffin pans, filling loaf pan halfway and muffin pan cups about two-thirds of the way to the top.

5 Bake the loaves for 50 minutes to 1 hour, or the muffins for 25 minutes, or until a toothpick inserted in the center comes out clean. Cool the loaf in the pan for at least one hour before turning out to cool completely.

Pineapple got name because it reminded people (and monsters) of pine cone. But it taste better!

39

Tip: For carrot biscuits, substitute ½ cup finely shredded carrot for the tomato and 1 teaspoon dried dill for the basil and oregano.

Bert's Whole-Wheat Tomato Drop Biscuits

Preparation time: 10 minutes • Baking time: 12 minutes • Makes 12 large biscuits

Warm out of the oven, these tender drop biscuits are so moist and tasty, they don't need butter or any other addition at the table.

Ingredients

- 1 cup whole-wheat flour
- 1 cup all-purpose flour
- ½ cup grated Parmesan cheese
- 1 tablespoon baking powder
- ½ teaspoon salt
- ½ teaspoon dried basil, crumbled
- ½ teaspoon dried oregano, crumbled
- 1 cup low-fat plain yogurt
- ⅓ cup olive oil
- 2 plum tomatoes or 1 large tomato, cored, seeded, and very finely chopped

Equipment

- Baking sheet
- Medium bowl
- Whisk
- Measuring cups
- Measuring spoons
- Rubber spatula
- Large bowl

1 Preheat the oven to 450°F. Lightly oil a baking sheet.

 2 Kids! In a medium bowl, whisk together the whole-wheat flour, all-purpose flour, Parmesan cheese, baking powder, salt, basil, and oregano.

3 In a large bowl, with spatula, stir together the yogurt and oil. Stir in the tomatoes. Stir the yogurt mixture into the flour mixture just until evenly moistened.

 4 Kids! Using a ¼-cup measuring cup, drop the dough onto the oiled baking sheet, leaving an inch of space between biscuits.

5 Bake 12 minutes or until tops just start to brown. Serve warm.

Scientifically speaking, tomatoes are fruits, because they have seeds inside them. But look for them in the vegetable aisle of your supermarket!

41

Tip: To make sweet biscuits for a strawberry shortcake–like dessert, add 1 tablespoon sugar to the flour mixture. If you like, you can also add 2 teaspoons grated lemon rind.

When biscuits are cool, split them open, top with a half-and-half combination of vanilla yogurt and whipped cream, and top the yogurt-cream with berries or cut-up fruit.

Abby Cadabby's
heavenly Biscuits

Preparation time: 15 minutes • Baking time: 12 minutes • Makes 12 biscuits

Cut these flaky biscuits out with star-shaped cutters so they really seem as if they dropped down from the heavens.

ingredients

- 1¾ cups all-purpose flour
- ¼ cup toasted wheat germ
- 1 tablespoon baking powder
- ¾ teaspoon salt
- ¾ cup low-fat plain yogurt
- ¼ cup olive oil

equipment

- Medium bowl
- Whisk
- Measuring cups
- Measuring spoons
- Large bowl
- Rubber spatula
- Cookie cutter (2-inch diameter)
- Baking sheet

1 Preheat the oven to 450°F.

 2 Kids! In a medium bowl, whisk together the flour, wheat germ, baking powder, and salt. In a large bowl, with a rubber spatula, stir together the yogurt and oil. Stir this into the flour mixture just until it is evenly moistened.

 3 Kids! Turn the dough out onto a lightly floured surface. With your fingers, gently pat the dough out to a ¼-inch-thick rectangle. Use a 2-inch cookie cutter to cut simple shapes such as triangles, hearts, or stars. Place the biscuits on an ungreased baking sheet about 1 inch apart.

4 Bake 10 to 12 minutes or until golden brown. Serve warm.

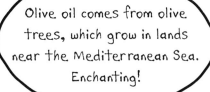

Olive oil comes from olive trees, which grow in lands near the Mediterranean Sea. Enchanting!

elmo's yummy tummy sweet potato biscuits

Preparation time: 20 minutes • Baking time: 12 minutes • Makes 12 biscuits

Sweet potatoes add some vitamin A and fiber to these pale orange biscuits. Serve warm with dinner, or have them for breakfast, split and filled with apple butter or a drizzle of honey.

Tips:

• For more sweetness, use a dark, intensely flavored honey such as buckwheat honey.

• To freeze, cut out and freeze before baking, the take out as many biscuits as you want to bake a one time. Let the biscuits stand on the baking she at room temperature while preheating the oven, then bake according to recipe directions.

ingredients

- 1 large sweet potato
- 1 cup all-purpose flour
- 1 cup whole-wheat flour
- ¼ cup cornmeal
- 1 tablespoon baking powder
- ¼ teaspoon salt
- 1 large egg
- ¼ cup olive oil
- ¼ cup low-fat (1%) milk
- 2 tablespoons honey

equipment

- Fork
- Microwave-safe plate
- Small bowl
- Wooden spoon
- Whisk
- Medium bowl
- Measuring cups
- Measuring spoons
- Rectangular pan (9×12-inch)
- Cooling rack

1 Prick the sweet potato all over with a fork and place on a microwave-safe plate. Microwave at High power for 8 minutes or until cooked through. Split potato open and set aside until cool enough to handle. Alternatively, peel the potato and cut into large chunks. In a saucepan, boil the chunks in enough water to cover for 20 minutes or until very tender. Drain and set potato chunks aside until cool.

 2 Scoop out or mash enough potato to measure 1 cup.

3 Preheat oven to 425°F.

 4 In a small bowl, whisk together all-purpose flour, whole-wheat flour, cornmeal, baking powder, and salt. In a medium bowl, with a wooden spoon, stir together egg, oil, milk, and honey. Stir in the sweet potato.

 5 Gradually add the flour mixture to the sweet potato mixture and stir until just combined.

6 Turn the dough out onto a lightly floured surface. With your fingers, gently pat the dough out to a 9x12-inch rectangle. Cut into 12 squares. Place biscuits on an ungreased baking sheet about 1 inch apart.

7 Bake 10 to 12 minutes or until golden brown. Cool slightly on rack and serve warm.

Elmo knows that many fruits and vegetables grow *above* the ground, but some—like potatoes, carrots, and radishes—grow *under* the ground.

main Dishes and sides

Baking is by no means limited to desserts and breakfast foods! In this chapter, you'll find savory pies, pockets, and "puffs" to serve as main dishes and side dishes for lunch, brunch, or dinner. On weekends, or whenever you have more time to spend in the kitchen, your children will love making their own pizza or calzone-type pockets, or hearty pot-pie-style main dishes, made with a

variety of classic doughs and crusts. On busier days, choose simpler dishes, such as Zoe's Tomato Tart, Oscar's Messy Green Stuff in a Potato Crust, or Big Bird's Crustless Veggie Quiche Squares. All of these recipes introduce young children to tasty new ways to enjoy a wide variety of fresh vegetables.

eLMO'S PiZZa ParTY

Preparation time: 20 minutes • Dough rising time: 1 hour • Baking time: 12 minutes
Makes 8 servings (2 pies; 16 small slices)

Pizza dough is a yeast dough, but pizza is essentially a flatbread, so rising is okay if you have time, but is not necessary. Try your favorite veggie, meat, and cheese toppings.

ingredients

Dough

- 1 cup lukewarm water (95-105°F)
- 1 teaspoon sugar
- 1 envelope (2½ teaspoons) active dry yeast
- 2½ cups all-purpose flour, plus extra for kneading
- ½ cup whole-wheat flour
- 1 teaspoon salt
- 1 tablespoon olive oil
- Yellow cornmeal

Topping

- 2 cups shredded, part-skim mozzarella
- 4 large, ripe tomatoes, thickly sliced
- 1 cup grated Parmesan cheese
- ½ cup chopped fresh basil or flat-leaf parsley

equipment

- Measuring cups
- Measuring spoons
- Glass measuring cup (1-cup)
- Food processor or large bowl
- Wooden spoon for stirring dough (optional)
- Pizza pans (two 12-inch)
- Cooling rack

1   In a 1-cup glass measuring cup, combine the water and sugar. Sprinkle yeast over mixture and let stand 5 minutes, or until frothy. Stir and let stand 5 minutes longer.

2   Meanwhile, in a food processor or large bowl, combine all-purpose flour, whole-wheat flour, and salt. Whirl or stir until mixed. Stir the oil into the dissolved yeast mixture. In the food processor, with motor running, add liquid mixture through the feed tube and process until mixture comes together into a slightly wet and sticky mass. Or in the bowl, make a well in the flour mixture, add liquid mixture, and stir to combine until a soft dough forms.

3 Kids!   With the help of an adult, turn the dough out onto a lightly floured surface and knead until smooth and elastic, 5 to 10 minutes. Divide dough into two flattened rounds of equal size. Let dough rest for at least 10 minutes,

or up to 1 hour. Or, if you want dough to rise, transfer to a clean, greased bowl, turning dough to grease all over. Cover with a kitchen towel and let the dough rise for 45 minutes. Punch the dough down, cover, and let rise 30 minutes longer.

4   Meanwhile, preheat the oven to 450°F.

5 Kids!   Sprinkle cornmeal on two 12-inch pizza pans. With the help of an adult, roll or press each round of dough out to a 12-inch round and transfer to pan.

6   Pre-bake each pie crust for 8 minutes or until lightly browned. Transfer the crust from the hot pan to a work surface to cool slightly. Leave the oven on.

7 Kids!   Sprinkle one-quarter of the mozzarella cheese evenly over each crust. Layer the tomatoes over the cheese. Sprinkle evenly with Parmesan and remaining mozzarella cheese. With the help of an adult, place the pizzas back on the pizza pans.

8   Bake for 8 to 10 minutes or until topping is heated through and the edge of the crust is browned. Transfer to cooling rack. Sprinkle with basil and let stand 5 minutes before cutting and serving.

Say "piece of pizza" five times fast. Wow! You're really good at that!

zoe's tomato tart

Preparation time: 15 minutes • Baking time: 20 minutes + 20 minutes standing time • Makes 6 servings

Adults will have to slice and chop the veggies and herbs, but since tortillas fill in for pie crust, and everything else is done by hand, this simple dish can be assembled almost entirely by children. They can truly say, "I made it myself!"

Tip: You can substitute thinly sliced mozzarella or provolone cheese for the Swiss in this recipe.

ingredients

- Olive oil for oiling pie plate
- 4 ripe medium-size tomatoes, thinly sliced
- 2 large (at least 8-inch) whole-wheat tortillas
- 1 tablespoon Dijon mustard
- 6 ounces thinly sliced Swiss or Jarlsberg cheese
- Salt and pepper, to taste
- ¼ cup chopped fresh basil
- 2 tablespoons chopped fresh parsley (optional)
- 1 green onion, white and green parts, trimmed and finely chopped

equipment

- Pie plate (9-inch)
- Paper towels
- Small spoon
- Pastry brush
- Small bowl
- Fork
- Cooling rack

1 Preheat the oven to 375°F.

2 With the help of an adult, lightly grease a 9-inch pie plate. Arrange the sliced tomatoes on several layers of paper towels to drain excess liquid.

3 Overlap the tortillas in the pie plate so they hang slightly over the edges of the plate. Spoon the mustard into the center. Use a pastry brush or the back of a spoon to "paint" the tortilla evenly with mustard.

4 Tear the cheese slices into large pieces. Make two layers each of cheese and tomatoes in the pie shell, alternating, starting with a layer of cheese and ending with a layer of tomatoes. Sprinkle with salt and pepper.

5 In a small bowl, combine the basil, parsley (if using), and green onion. Sprinkle evenly over the tomatoes.

6 Bake 20 minutes or until cheese is melted. Transfer to rack to cool for at least 20 minutes before slicing into wedges and serving. Serve warm or at room temperature.

What can you find in your kitchen that is round like a tortilla?

grover's Roasted Ratatouille Pie

Preparation time: 45 minutes • Baking time: 42 minutes • Makes 6 servings

Guess how the the eggplant got its name! It is sort of egg-shaped, and comes in many colors, including white.

This open-face vegetable pie is a hearty and satisfying vegetarian main dish to serve for lunch, brunch, or dinner.

ingredients

Cornmeal Crust

- ¼ cup ice-cold water
- 1 egg yolk
- 1 teaspoon cider vinegar
- 1½ cups all-purpose flour
- ½ cup cornmeal
- ¼ teaspoon salt
- ¼ teaspoon baking powder
- 2 tablespoons chilled butter, cut up
- ¼ cup olive oil, frozen for at least one hour in advance, or until semi-solid

Filling

- 2 medium tomatoes, trimmed and cut into ¼-inch-thick slices
- 1 small eggplant, trimmed and cut into ¼-inch-thick slices
- 1 medium zucchini, trimmed and cut into ¼-inch-thick slices
- 1 large clove garlic, thinly sliced
- 2 tablespoons olive oil
- ¼ teaspoon salt
- ½ teaspoon each dried rosemary and thyme, crumbled
- ½ cup shredded mozzarella cheese

equipment

- Small bowl
- Measuring cups
- Measuring spoons
- Fork
- Medium bowl
- Whisk
- Pastry blender
- Large baking dish
- Wooden spoon

1 Preheat the oven to 425°F.

 2 Kids! In a small bowl, stir together the water, egg yolk, and vinegar until well-blended. Place the bowl in the refrigerator. In a medium bowl, whisk together the flour, cornmeal, salt, and baking powder until well-mixed.

3 Use a pastry blender to cut the butter and frozen oil into the flour mixture until coarse crumbs form. Take the egg mixture out of the refrigerator. Slowly add the mixture to the flour crumbs and toss with a fork until the dough sticks together. (If the dough is too wet, add a little extra flour.)

"Ratatouille" comes from a French word that means to toss or stir. Can you find France on a map or globe?

 4 Kids! With the help of an adult, roll dough out on a lightly floured surface or pastry cloth to make an 11-inch circle. Transfer the dough to a 9-inch pie plate. Crimp the dough around the edges of the pie. Use a fork to gently prick holes all over the bottom of the crust.

5 Bake for 12 minutes. Set pie crust aside and leave oven on.

 6 Kids! Meanwhile, in a baking dish large enough to hold the vegetables in a single layer, use a wooden spoon to gently toss the tomatoes, eggplant, zucchini, and garlic in olive oil. Sprinkle the vegetables with salt, rosemary, and thyme and toss again.

7 Roast the vegetables for 10 minutes, gently stirring once halfway through cooking. Reduce oven temperature to 350°F. Spoon the vegetables into the precooked pie crust.

 8 Kids! Sprinkle the mozzarella cheese evenly over the vegetables.

9 Bake 20 minutes or until cheese is melted and pie is heated through.

Tip: You can make and pre-bake the crust ahead of time; refrigerate or freeze until you are ready to fill and bake the pie.

Rosita's
Beefy Enchilada Pie

Preparation time: 30 minutes • Baking time: 40 minutes • Makes 6 servings

This is a mild dish, so if your family likes Mexican food hot and spicy, use a diced tomato product or a variety of cheese that contains chile peppers.

Ingredients

Double Corn Crust

- 1 can (8 ounces) sweet corn kernels, drained and rinsed

- 1 tablespoon olive oil

- ⅔ cup finely ground cornmeal

- ½ teaspoon salt

- ½ cup boiling water

- ½ cup (2 ounces) shredded Monterey Jack cheese

Filling

- 1 tablespoon olive oil

- 1 onion, finely chopped

- 1 sweet green or red pepper, finely chopped

- ½ pound lean ground beef

- ½ teaspoon salt

- 1 cup (4 ounces) shredded reduced-fat Cheddar, Monterey Jack, or pepper jack cheese, or Tex-Mex cheese blend

- 1 cup drained, rinsed pinto beans or black beans

- 1 can (14 ounces) diced tomatoes with onion and garlic or jalapeño peppers

Equipment

- Measuring cups

- Measuring spoons

- Large bowls (2)

- Fork

- Rubber spatula

- Deep-dish pie plate (9-inch)

- Large spoon

- Large skillet

- Cooling rack

Suggested Toppings

Reduced-fat plain Greek-style yogurt or reduced-fat sour cream, finely chopped green or red onions, sliced green or ripe olives, chopped fresh cilantro, chopped fresh tomato, avocado cubes

1. Preheat the oven to 350°F. Lightly grease a 9-inch deep-dish pie plate or shallow casserole.

2. **Kids!** In a large bowl, stir together the corn, olive oil, cornmeal, and salt.

3. Add boiling water to the bowl and stir to mix well. Stir in the Monterey Jack cheese. Set aside to cool slightly.

4. **Kids!** With the help of an adult, use a rubber spatula to spread the corn mixture evenly across the bottom and up the side of the pie plate to form a crust.

5. Bake the crust for 15 minutes. Transfer to rack to cool slightly while making filling. Leave the oven on.

6. In a large skillet, heat the oil over medium heat. Add the onion and sauté 3 minutes. Add the peppers and sauté 2 minutes longer. Stir in the ground meat and salt. Cook, stirring often, until meat is browned. Set aside to cool slightly.

7. **Kids!** In another large bowl, mix the beans, tomatoes, and ½ cup of the Cheddar cheese. With the help of an adult, stir in the cooled meat mixture and spoon this mixture into the pie plate. Sprinkle the remaining ½ cup cheese evenly over the top.

8. Bake for 25 minutes or until mixture is thoroughly heated and cheese is melted. Transfer the pie to a cooling rack for 5 minutes before slicing into wedges.

Tip: You can substitute ground pork, chicken, or turkey for the beef in this recipe.

The number of the day is 1: 1 can of corn, 1 onion, 1 pepper, 1 cup of cheese, and 1 can of beans. Ah, how I love the number 1! (That's uno in Spanish.)

OSCAR'S MESSY GREEN STUFF IN A POTATO CRUST

Preparation time: 10 minutes • Baking time: 20 minutes • Makes 4 to 6 servings

A layer of pre-baked, sliced potatoes takes the place of traditional crust. For a messy meaty pie, add a cup of finely diced lean ham to the filling.

Ingredients

- 1 tablespoon olive oil

- 1 large or 2 medium Yukon gold or all-purpose potatoes, peeled and sliced ⅛-inch thick

- 8 cups kale or spinach leaves

- 1 small onion, finely chopped (½ cup)

- 3 eggs

- 1 cup low-fat cottage cheese

- ⅓ cup grated Parmesan cheese

- 1 teaspoon dried rosemary, crushed

- 1 medium tomato, cored, seeded, and finely chopped

Equipment

- Measuring cups

- Measuring spoons

- Vegetable peeler

- Pie plate (9-inch)

- Large skillet

- Large bowl

- Fork

- Large spoon

- Cooling rack

56

1. Preheat the oven to 350°F. Use 1 teaspoon of the olive oil to coat the pie plate.

2. **Kids!** Line the bottom of the pie plate with one layer of potato slices. Ask an adult to cut the remaining slices in half to fit up and around the side of the plate.

3. Pre-bake the potato crust for 15 minutes. Transfer the pie plate to a rack until it is cool enough to handle. Leave the oven on.

4. **Kids!** Meanwhile, use your hands to tear the kale or spinach leaves into small pieces.

5. In a large skillet, heat the remaining 2 teaspoons of oil over medium heat. Add the onion and sauté, stirring occasionally, for 5 minutes. Add the spinach and cook, stirring often, for 2 minutes or until wilted. Pour mixture into a sieve or colander to drain; set aside.

6. In a large bowl, stir together the eggs, cottage cheese, Parmesan cheese, and rosemary until well-mixed. Stir in the cooled spinach mixture.

7. **Kids!** With the help of an adult, spoon the spinach and cheese mixture over the potatoes in the pie plate, spreading evenly. Sprinkle evenly with chopped tomato.

8. Bake 20 to 25 minutes or until filling is set and a toothpick inserted near the center of the pie comes out clean. Transfer to a rack to cool slightly. Cut into wedges and serve.

Tip: You can substitute part-skim ricotta or farmer cheese for the cottage cheese in this recipe, or use a mixture.

The messier, the better!

I ♥ trash!

elmo's Chicken pot pie

Preparation time: 25 minutes • Baking time: 30 minutes • Makes 4 servings

ingredients

Filling

- 1 cup cremini or white button mushrooms, stems removed
- 1 tablespoon olive oil
- 1 onion, finely chopped
- 1 carrot, peeled and finely chopped
- 1 small stalk celery, thinly sliced
- 1 small potato, such as Yukon Gold, peeled and finely diced
- 2 tablespoons all-purpose flour
- ¾ cup vegetable broth or bouillon
- ¾ cup low-fat milk
- 1 cup diced cooked chicken
- ½ cup frozen petit peas, thawed
- ½ cup frozen corn kernels, thawed

Buttermilk Biscuit Topping

- ½ cup all-purpose flour

- ¼ cup whole-wheat flour
- ½ teaspoon baking powder
- ¼ teaspoon baking soda
- ¼ teaspoon salt
- 1 tablespoon cold butter, cut into pieces
- ¼ cup grated Parmesan cheese (optional)
- ½ cup buttermilk
- 2 teaspoons olive oil

equipment

- Plastic knife
- Large saucepan
- Measuring cups
- Measuring spoons
- Vegetable peeler
- Whisk
- Spoon for stirring
- Baking dish (1½-quart)
- Large bowl
- Big spoon
- Cooling rack

Get your children involved in the vegetable preparation. Older children can use a plastic knife to slice the mushrooms, while younger children can use their fingers to break the mushroom caps apart.

1 Preheat the oven to 400°F.

 2 With the help of an adult, use a plastic knife to slice the mushrooms, or use your fingers to simply break them into small pieces.

3 Heat the oil in a large saucepan over medium heat. Add the onion and sauté 2 minutes. Add the carrots and celery and cook 5 minutes longer. Stir in the potatoes and cook 5 minutes longer. Stir in the mushrooms and cook 3 minutes longer.

4 Sprinkle the flour over the vegetables and stir to dissolve. Cook for 2 minutes, stirring occasionally. Slowly stir the broth and milk into the vegetable mixture in the saucepan until a smooth sauce forms. Cook over low heat, stirring often, for 5 minutes or until the sauce is thickened. Remove from heat and stir in the chicken, peas, and corn. Pour the mixture into a 1½-quart baking dish.

 5 In a large bowl, whisk together the all-purpose flour, whole-wheat flour, baking powder, baking soda, and salt. Add the butter pieces and use your fingers to mix the butter into the flour mixture until crumbly. With a spoon, stir in the Parmesan cheese, if using. Stir in the buttermilk and oil just until mixed.

6 Use a big spoon to scoop up the biscuit dough and drop it on top of the vegetable filling, all around the edges of the baking dish.

7 Place the baking dish on a baking sheet. Bake 30 minutes, or until biscuit topping is golden brown and filling is bubbly. Transfer to rack for 10 minutes to cool slightly before serving.

Tip: To make individual pot pies, use 12-ounce ramekins or ovenproof bowls. Divide the filling evenly among the bowls, top each with a scoop of biscuit topping, and bake as directed, checking after 25 minutes.

Do the chicken dance with Elmo! Flap your wings and cluck like a chicken!

Bert's sausage pockets with tomato dipping sauce

Preparation time: 30 minutes • Baking time: 25 minutes • Makes 6 pockets

ingredients

Spinach Dough

- 1 cup lukewarm water (95° to 105°F)
- 1 envelope (2½ teaspoons) active dry yeast
- 2 teaspoons sugar
- 3¼ cups bread flour or all-purpose flour, plus extra for kneading
- ¼ cup cornmeal
- 1 teaspoon salt
- 2 tablespoons olive oil
- 2 cups raw spinach leaves, very finely chopped (⅔ cup)

Filling

- 1 container (15 ounces) part-skim ricotta cheese
- 2 cups (8 ounces) shredded part-skim mozzarella cheese
- ½ cup grated Parmesan cheese

- ½ teaspoon dried basil, crushed
- Pinch of nutmeg
- 3 large links (about 10 ounces) turkey sausage, cooked and thinly sliced
- ¼ cup low-fat milk, for glazing dough
- 1½ cups marinara or other tomato sauce, for dipping

equipment

- Measuring cups
- Measuring spoons
- Large bowl
- Wooden spoon
- Kitchen towel
- Medium bowl
- Rolling pin
- Baking sheet
- Fork
- Cooling rack

A fun meal in a pocket and healthy, too—the greens are in the crust!

Tip: To save time, you can use a pound of refrigerated or thawed frozen pizza dough. Knead in the finely chopped spinach and continue as directed in the recipe.

Pour the warm water into a large bowl. Sprinkle the yeast and sugar over the water. Let stand 5 to 10 minutes, or until foamy.

 With a wooden spoon, stir 1 cup of the flour, cornmeal, salt, and olive oil into the yeast mixture until well-mixed. Stir in the spinach. Stir in the remaining flour, ½ cup at a time, mixing completely to make a soft dough. Let a grown-up help with the stirring when the dough starts to get stiff.

3 Turn the dough out onto a lightly floured work surface. Knead 5 to 10 minutes, or until smooth and elastic, adding more flour if necessary to prevent dough from sticking to the work surface. Cover the dough with a kitchen towel or large bowl and let rest for at least 15 minutes.

 Preheat the oven to 400°F.

 In a medium bowl, stir together the ricotta, mozzarella, and Parmesan cheeses, basil, and nutmeg until well-mixed.

 With the help of an adult, divide the dough into six equal pieces. Roll each piece into a ball and flatten with your hands. On a lightly floured surface with a lightly floured rolling pin, roll each ball out to a circle 8 inches in diameter.

7 Spoon the cheese filling in the center of each round of dough, dividing evenly. Top with sausage. With the help of an adult, fold the dough over the filling to form a half-moon shape. Fold the edge of the dough over and press the edge all around with a fork to seal tightly. Transfer pockets to a baking sheet. Use a fork to gently poke several tiny holes in the top of each pocket. Use a pastry brush to lightly "paint" each calzone with milk.

8 Bake for 20 to 25 minutes or until golden brown. Transfer to rack and let cool for 15 minutes. Cut each pocket in half and let stand until filling has cooled considerably but is still warm. Meanwhile, gently heat up tomato sauce and serve ¼ cup in a small bowl with each calzone, for dipping.

Hey Ernie! What did the baker say to the dough?

I KNEAD you! Hee, hee, hee!

cookie monster's veggie turnovers

Preparation time: 40 minutes • Baking time: 20 minutes • Makes 6 servings

This is a great way to get your kids to eat greens—put 'em in a pocket! You can fill these turnovers with any precooked or leftover vegetables you choose and vary the type of cheese you use.

ingredients

Cream Cheese Pastry

- 1½ cups all-purpose flour
- ½ cup whole-wheat flour
- ½ teaspoon salt
- ½ cup (1 stick) butter
- 1 package (3 ounces) reduced-fat cream cheese
- 2 to 3 tablespoons ice cold water

Filling

- 2 tablespoons olive oil
- 1 onion, finely chopped (1 cup)
- 3 small Yukon gold or all-purpose potatoes, peeled and cut into ½-inch dice
- ½ teaspoon salt
- 2 cups finely chopped greens such as kale, Swiss chard, arugula, spinach, or mustard greens, well rinsed
- ¼ cup finely chopped roasted red pepper
- 2 cloves garlic, finely chopped
- 2 ounces shredded part-skim mozzarella cheese
- 2 ounces goat cheese or crumbled feta cheese
- 1 egg

equipment

- Measuring cups
- Measuring spoons
- Medium bowl
- Whisk
- Pastry blender
- Vegetable peeler
- Large skillet
- Large bowl
- Rolling pin
- Fork
- Baking sheet
- Small bowl
- Cooling rack

Tip: For a meaty turnover, replace the feta cheese with up to ½ cup chopped lean ham, cooked turkey bacon, or any leftover cooked meat or poultry, including ground meat.

1 In a medium bowl, whisk together the all-purpose flour, whole-wheat flour, and salt.

 2 With the help of an adult, use a pastry blender to cut the butter into the flour mixture until the mixture is in coarse crumbs. Add the cream cheese and 2 tablespoons water and stir until pastry comes together in a ball.

 3 Leave the dough in the bowl and press down into a flattened round. Cover and refrigerate while preparing filling.

 4 In a large skillet, heat the oil over medium heat. Add the onion and sauté for 3 minutes. Add the potatoes and salt, reduce heat to medium low, cover and cook for 10 minutes.

5 Stir the greens, roasted pepper, and garlic into the skillet. Cook 5 minutes. Spoon the vegetable mixture into a large bowl and set aside to cool.

6 Preheat the oven to 400°F.

7 Sprinkle your work surface lightly with flour. With the help of an adult, divide the dough into 6 equal pieces. With a floured rolling pin, roll each piece out to a 6- or 8-inch circle.

 8 Spoon the potato mixture evenly into the center of each round. Top with a spoonful of mozzarella and goat cheese.

 9 With the help of an adult, fold dough over the filling to form a half-moon shape. Fold the edge of the dough over and press the edge all around, crimping with a fork to seal tightly.

10 Use a fork to gently prick several sets of holes into each turnover. Place the turnovers on an ungreased baking sheet. In a small bowl, beat the egg until smooth. Use a pastry brush to "paint" each turnover with a little beaten egg.

11 Bake for 20 minutes or until golden brown. Transfer to rack and let cool for 15 minutes. Cut each pocket in half and serve warm.

Me cannot believe it! Clothes can have pockets, animals like kangaroos and koalas can have pockets, now even food can have pockets. What next?!

Abby Cadabby's
Amazing Carrot Puff

Preparation time: 25 minutes • Baking time: 40 minutes • Makes 4 to 6 servings

This light carrot pudding puffs up in the oven, then deflates slightly when you bring it to the table—something like an old-fashioned soufflé. Serve as a light main dish for lunch or brunch or as a side dish with chicken, turkey, or other meats for dinner.

ingredients

- 5 medium carrots, peeled and thinly sliced
- 2 tablespoons olive oil
- 2 tablespoons very finely chopped onion
- 2 tablespoons all-purpose flour
- ½ teaspoon salt
- ⅛ teaspoon pepper
- ⅛ teaspoon ground nutmeg
- 1 cup low-fat milk
- 3 eggs, separated

equipment

- Measuring cups
- Measuring spoons
- Vegetable peeler
- Medium saucepan
- Colander
- Large bowl
- Potato masher
- Medium bowl
- Electric mixer
- Wooden spoon
- Baking dish (1-quart)
- Cooling rack

1 Preheat the oven to 350°F.

2 In a medium saucepan, boil or steam the carrots for 8 to 10 minutes until very tender. Drain and transfer carrots to a large bowl and set aside to cool slightly.

3 In the same saucepan, heat the oil over medium heat. Add the onion and sauté 5 minutes, or until tender. Stir in the flour, salt, pepper, and nutmeg until well-blended. Remove from heat. Slowly stir in the milk. Return the saucepan to the heat and cook, stirring, until thickened. Set aside to cool slightly.

 4 With the help of an adult, in a large bowl, use a potato masher to mash the carrots until smooth. Stir in the egg yolks until well-blended. Gradually stir in the milk mixture.

5 With an electric mixer at medium-high speed, beat the egg whites in a medium bowl until stiff peaks form.

 6 With a wooden spoon, stir ½ cup of the beaten egg whites into the carrot mixture.

7 Gently fold in the remaining whites just until blended. Turn the mixture into an ungreased 1-quart baking dish.

8 Bake for 35 to 40 minutes or until top is golden brown and set in the center. Transfer to rack for 5 minutes before serving.

Carrots are root vegetables. That means they grow under the ground, like beets and radishes.

Tip: To serve as an appetizer or as finger-food for a party, cut each large quiche square into 4 equal smaller squares for a total of 16 squares.

Big Bird's crustless veggie quiche squares

Preparation time: 20 minutes • Baking time: 45 minutes

Makes 4 main-dish servings or 16 appetizer-size servings

Quiche is much lower in fat (and calories) when the crust is eliminated.

ingredients

- 1 teaspoon olive oil
- 1 large onion, finely chopped
- 1 large zucchini, shredded
- ½ teaspoon salt
- 2 large eggs
- ¼ cup milk
- 3 carrots, peeled and grated
- 1 cup shredded Swiss or Gruyère cheese
- 1 tablespoon chopped fresh dill or 1 teaspoon dried dill

equipment

- 8-inch baking pan
- Measuring cups
- Measuring spoons
- Grater
- Large nonstick skillet
- Large bowl
- Fork
- Vegetable peeler
- Wooden spoon
- Cooling rack

> Count the sides on the veggie quiche square. What else can you find in your kitchen that's square-shaped?

1. Heat oven to 375°F. Lightly grease an 8-inch square baking pan with nonstick cooking spray.

2. Heat oil in large nonstick skillet over medium heat. Add onion; sauté 3 minutes. Stir in zucchini. Increase heat to medium-high and sauté until zucchini is tender and all liquid in skillet has evaporated, about 8 minutes. Stir in ¼ teaspoon of the salt.

3. **kids!** In large bowl, with the help of an adult, use a fork to beat together the eggs and milk. When blended, add zucchini mixture, carrots, cheese, dill, and remaining ¼ teaspoon salt. Use a wooden spoon to mix all the ingredients together. Spread the mixture in the prepared pan.

4. Bake until center is just set, about 45 minutes. Transfer the pan to a wire rack to cool for 10 to 15 minutes before cutting. Cut into 4 equal squares. Serve warm or at room temperature.

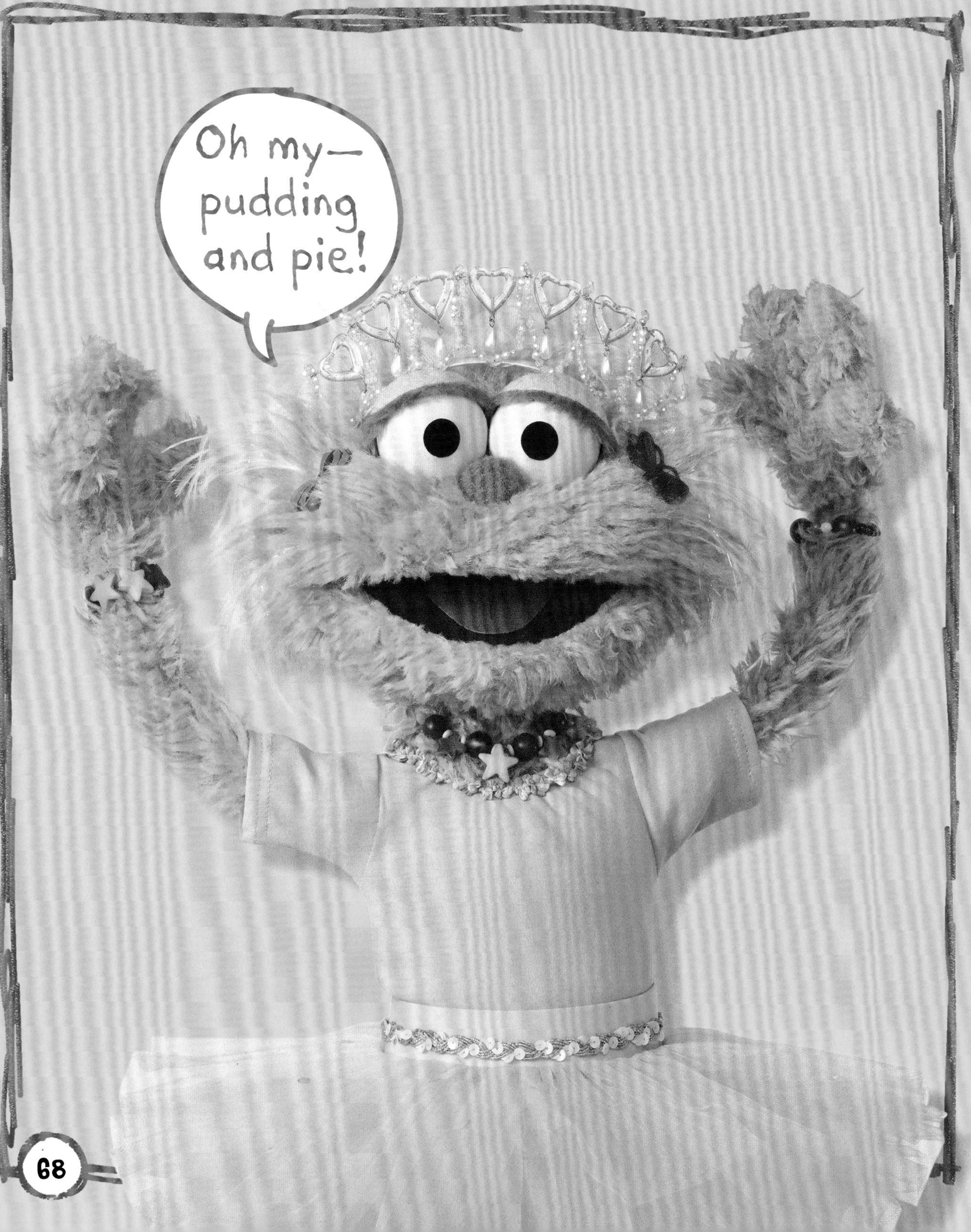
Oh my—
pudding
and pie!

puddings and pies

By baking classic rice pudding, pumpkin pudding, and noodle pudding, children learn that many foods, from rice and pasta to fruits and vegetables, can be used to make both side dishes for lunch and supper and tasty desserts and snacks. Best of all, they learn that pudding is much more than a sweet powder poured from a box.

Pies and tarts can also be made healthier by skipping the traditional high-fat pastry crust and

choosing fillings and toppings with less fat or sugar. An old-fashioned fruit crumble is a wonderful alternative to a traditional pie. It has no crust at all, but its crunchy-sweet oat topping more than equals a crust in both flavor and texture.

ernie's
corny corn pudding

Preparation time: 20 minutes • Baking time: 35 minutes • Makes 4 servings

This recipe is based on a classic southern recipe, but with the traditional spoonful of sugar eliminated and the butter replaced with olive oil. It is delicious served with baked ham for dinner, smoked turkey for lunch, or turkey bacon for breakfast or brunch.

Here's a corny joke for you: don't tell secrets in a cornfield. There are too many ears listening!

ingredients

- 1 can (14 to 15 ounces) sweet corn kernels, drained and rinsed
- ⅓ cup low-fat (1%) milk
- 3 eggs, separated
- 3 tablespoons olive oil
- ⅓ cup all-purpose flour
- ½ teaspoon salt
- ½ teaspoon baking powder
- ½ cup (2 ounces) shredded Cheddar cheese
- ¼ cup chopped sweet green or red pepper (or a mix)

equipment

- Measuring cups
- Measuring spoons
- Baking dish (1½-quart)
- Food processor or blender
- Measuring cups
- Measuring spoons
- Medium bowls (2)
- Electric mixer
- Whisk
- Rubber spatula
- Cooling rack

1 Preheat the oven to 350°F. Lightly oil a 1½-quart baking dish.

2 In a food processor or blender, combine half the corn kernels and the milk. Whirl until mixture is a smooth puree.

3 kids! With the machine running and the top in place, add the yolks through the food shoot, one at a time. Process until each yolk is fully incorporated.

4 With the machine still running, add the oil and continue processing until fully incorporated.

5 kids! In a medium bowl, whisk together the flour, salt, and baking powder. Stir in the corn mixture and shredded cheese. Stir in the remaining corn kernels.

6 In a clean medium bowl, with an electric mixer at medium-high speed, beat the egg whites just until soft peaks form. Fold the whites into the corn mixture. With a rubber spatula, scrape batter into the oiled baking dish.

7 Sprinkled chopped sweet pepper over the top of the corn mixture.

8 Bake 35 minutes or until golden brown on top and barely set in center. Transfer to rack to cool slightly (Pudding will deflate as it cools.) Serve warm or at room temperature.

Tip: For maximum flavor, opt for sharp or extra-sharp Cheddar cheese.

Well-mannered furry blue monsters always say "Bon Appetit!" at mealtime. In French that means, "Enjoy your delicious food!"

grover's Cherry Clafouti

Preparation time: 20 minutes • Baking time: 25 minutes • Makes 6 servings

A clafouti (cla-foo-tee) is a cross between a pudding and pancake, from the country of France. While it is most often served for dessert, it's also good for breakfast or brunch.

Ingredients

- 4 large eggs
- 1 cup low-fat milk
- ½ cup all-purpose flour
- ⅓ cup granulated sugar
- ¼ cup wheat germ
- 1 teaspoon vanilla extract
- ¼ teaspoon almond extract (optional)
- ⅛ teaspoon salt
- 1 pint (2 cups) pitted sweet cherries, such as Bing
- Confectioner's sugar (optional)

Equipment

- Pie plate (10-inch) or 6 ramekins (6 ounces each)
- Large bowl
- Whisk
- Measuring cups
- Measuring spoons
- Toothpick
- Cooling rack
- Fine-mesh strainer

Tip: Cherries are traditional in a clafouti, but you can substitute an equal amount of raspberries, blueberries, peach, fig, or nectarine halves, or other berries or soft cut-up fruit. To use apples, pears, or other hard fruit in this recipe, slice and sauté first in a little bit of butter mixed with olive oil, or steam over simmering water in a covered pot for a few minutes to soften slightly.

1 Preheat the oven to 400°F. Lightly grease a 10-inch pie plate or shallow baking dish. To make individual cups of clafouti, grease six 6-ounce ramekins or custard cups.

 2 Kids! In a large bowl, whisk together the eggs, milk, flour, granulated sugar, wheat germ, vanilla, almond extract, if using, and salt until well-blended. With the help of an adult, pour half the mixture into the prepared baking dish. Sprinkle the cherries evenly over the batter. Carefully pour the remaining batter over the cherries.

3 Bake for 20 to 25 minutes or until puffed and golden brown around the edges and a toothpick inserted in the center comes out clean. Transfer to rack to cool slightly. To bake individual cups, bake for 15 minutes or until a toothpick inserted in the center comes out clean.

 4 Kids! If you wish, just before serving, and when the baking dish is cool enough to touch, sprinkle the clafouti with a touch of confectioner's sugar through a fine-mesh strainer.

5 Cut into wedges and serve warm.

Tips:

• To make individual servings, divide the pudding between eight 6-ounce custard cups before baking. Bake 25 minutes or until centers are just firm.

• Pumpkin Pudding is delicious with pineapple or steamed pear or apple slices.

cookie monster's pumpkin pudding

Preparation time: 15 minutes • Baking time: 45 minutes • Makes 8 servings

This tastes like a light pumpkin pie, but with a touch of real maple syrup and without a crust. You can bake the pudding in a small casserole dish for a homey dessert or snack, or in individual custard cups or ramekins, to dress it up for special occasions.

ingredients

- 3 large eggs
- 1 can (15 ounces) pumpkin puree
- ¾ cup packed light brown sugar
- ¼ cup real maple syrup
- 1½ teaspoons pumpkin pie spice
- 2 cups low-fat milk

equipment

- Baking dish (1-quart)
- Medium bowl
- Whisk
- Measuring cups
- Measuring spoons
- Cooling rack

1 Preheat the oven to 350°F. Lightly grease a 1-quart baking dish.

2 Kids! In a medium bowl, whisk together the eggs, pumpkin, brown sugar, maple syrup, and pie spice. With the help of an adult, gradually pour in the milk and continue whisking until the mixture is smooth. Pour the mixture into the prepared baking dish.

3 Bake for 45 minutes or until center is just set. Transfer to rack to cool. Serve warm, or refrigerate and serve cold.

Maple syrup come from sap of maple tree. Native Americans were first people known to collect sap from trees and use in cooking. Mmmm, sticky and sweet!

Tips:
- To add crunch, sprinkle whole-grain granola or crushed corn flakes over the top before baking.

- Serve noodle pudding on its own or with applesauce or fresh sliced fruit or berries on the side.

Elmo's Cinnamon-y Sweet Noodle-Doodle Pudding

Preparation time: 15 minutes plus 15 minutes stovetop cooking time
Baking time: 45 minutes • Makes 4 to 6 servings

Noodle pudding can be savory or sweet. The classic recipe uses creamed cottage cheese and sour cream. This lightened-up version uses part-skim ricotta cheese and low-fat Greek style yogurt instead, but tastes just as rich and sweet. Serve sweet noodle pudding as a side dish for breakfast or brunch or as a dessert or snack.

ingredients

- **2 cups uncooked medium-wide noodles (about 5 ounces)**
- **2 tablespoons olive oil**
- **4 large eggs**
- **1 cup part-skim ricotta cheese**
- **1 cup low-fat plain Greek-style yogurt**
- **⅓ cup sugar**
- **½ teaspoon ground cinnamon**
- **⅓ cup golden or dark seedless raisins**

equipment

- **Baking dish (1-quart) or baking pan (8-inch square)**
- **Large saucepan**
- **Large bowl**
- **Whisk**
- **Measuring cups**
- **Measuring spoons**
- **Wooden spoon**
- **Cooling rack**

1 Preheat the oven to 350°F. Lightly grease a 1-quart baking dish or 8-inch-square baking pan.

2 In a large saucepan of boiling water, cook the noodles according to package directions until tender. Drain in a colander and toss with the oil.

3 Kids! In a large bowl, whisk together the eggs, ricotta cheese, yogurt, sugar, and cinnamon. With a wooden spoon, stir in the drained noodles and raisins. Spoon the mixture into the oiled baking dish.

4 Bake 45 minutes or until the mixture is set in the center and lightly browned on top. Transfer to rack to cool before serving.

How I love noodles—let me count the ways. There's macaroni, rigatoni. . . . Count the different noodles you see in your pantry, or on your next trip to the market!

Zoe's Baked Brown Rice Pudding

Preparation time: 45 minutes • Baking time: 1 hour 30 minutes • Makes 6 servings

Pop this chewy-sweet pudding into the oven before you prepare dinner, and it will be ready just in time for dessert.

Tips:

• You can use any type of brown rice in this recipe, but medium-grain gives the pudding the best consistency.

• The brown sugar and raisins add plenty of sweetness so if you want to serve this rice pudding with fruit, try something tart or tangy, such as orange sections, chunks of kiwi, or thinly sliced plums.

ingredients

- ½ cup raw medium-grain brown rice

- ⅓ cup packed light brown sugar

- ¼ teaspoon ground cinnamon

- ⅛ teaspoon ground nutmeg

- ⅛ teaspoon salt

- ¼ cup golden raisins

- 1½ cups low-fat milk

- 1 can (12 ounces) low-fat (2%) evaporated milk

- 1 teaspoon vanilla extract

equipment

- Medium saucepan

- Baking pan (11×7×2-inch or 2-quart baking dish)

- Measuring cups

- Measuring spoons

- Spoon for stirring

- Colander or large strainer

- Wooden spoon

- Cooling rack

1 In a medium saucepan, cover the rice with 2 cups water. Heat to a boil over medium-high heat; reduce heat to low and simmer, uncovered, for 40 minutes.

 2 Kids! Meanwhile, in an 11x7x2-inch baking pan or other 2-quart baking dish, stir together the brown sugar, cinnamon, nutmeg, and salt. Stir in the raisins.

3 Preheat the oven to 300°F. Drain the cooked rice into a colander or large sieve. Cool slightly.

 4 Kids! With a wooden spoon, stir the rice into the sugar mixture in the baking dish.

5 Wipe out the saucepan used to cook the rice and add regular low-fat milk and evaporated milk. Heat just to a boil over medium-high heat. Remove from heat and stir in the vanilla. Pour over the rice mixture.

6 Bake for 45 minutes. Stir well and continue to bake until rice is tender and browned on top, 30 to 45 minutes longer. Transfer to rack to cool slightly. Scoop into dessert cups and serve warm or cool completely and refrigerate to serve cold.

What words can you think of that rhyme with rice?

Abby Cadabby's
magic Lemon pudding cake

Preparation time: 20 minutes • Baking time: 1 hour • Makes 6 servings

As if by magic, this batter separates in the oven, forming a pudding-like sauce on the bottom and a thin, sponge cake–like layer on top. This is one old-fashioned dessert that never gets old!

Tip: You can use equal amounts of lime rind and lime juice or a mixture of lemon and lime to make this pudding cake.

ingredients

- 3 large eggs, separated
- ¾ cup sugar
- 2 tablespoons butter, softened
- ¼ cup fresh lemon juice
- 2 teaspoons grated lemon rind
- ⅛ teaspoon salt
- ¼ cup all-purpose flour
- 1 cup whole milk or 2% reduced-fat
- Blueberries, raspberries, or strawberries (optional)

equipment

- **Baking dish (1-quart)**
- **Small bowl**
- **Medium bowl**
- **Electric mixer**
- **Measuring cups**
- **Measuring spoons**
- **Rubber spatula**
- **Baking pan (13×9×2-inch)**
- **Cooling rack**

1 Preheat the oven to 350°F. Lightly grease a 1-quart baking dish.

 2 In a small bowl, with the help of an adult and with perfectly clean beaters, beat the egg whites just until stiff peaks form. Set aside while preparing the batter.

 3 In a medium bowl, with the help of an adult and with an electric mixer, beat together the sugar and butter. Add the egg yolks and beat until well-blended. Beat in the lemon juice, lemon rind, and salt. Beat in the flour, alternately with the milk, until well-mixed. Using a rubber spatula, gently fold in the beaten egg whites.

 4 Pour the batter into the prepared baking dish.

5 Place a 13x9x2-inch baking pan in the oven and carefully fill with 1 inch of hot water. Carefully place the pudding dish in the larger dish.

6 Bake for 1 hour or until the cake-like top that forms is set. Carefully transfer the pudding cake to a rack and let stand at least 30 minutes. Serve warm or cold.

 7 After an adult scoops out the pudding cake onto plates, add a few berries to each plate before serving, if you like.

Most eggs have just one yoke inside, but every once in a while, there are two. And that's no yoke!

81

Oscar's
Crumbly Apple Crumble

Preparation time: 20 minutes • Baking time: 40 minutes • Makes 4 to 6 servings

A crumble is a fruit pie with a sweet and "crumbly" oatmeal or multi-grain topping instead of a crust. Serve warm, if you like, topped with a small scoop of vanilla ice cream or frozen yogurt.

Tip: The sweeter the apples you choose, the sweeter the crumble. Combining apple varieties gives the crumble a good mix of flavors and textures.

ingredients

Topping

- 1½ cups uncooked old-fashioned oats or multi-grain flakes used for hot cereal

- ½ cup packed light brown sugar

- ¼ cup all-purpose flour

- ¼ cup (½ stick) butter

Filling

- 2 pounds baking apples such as Fuji, Jonagold, or Granny Smith, or a mix, peeled, halved, cored, and sliced thickly

- 1 tablespoon lemon juice

- 1 teaspoon ground cinnamon

- ¼ teaspoon ground nutmeg

- ⅛ teaspoon ground cloves

equipment

- **Medium bowl**

- **Measuring cups**

- **Measuring spoons**

- **Large bowl**

- **Wooden spoon**

- **Pie plate (9- or 10-inch)**

- **Cooling rack**

1 Preheat the oven to 350°F.

 2 In a medium bowl, combine the oats or grain flakes, brown sugar, and flour. Add the butter and use your fingers to rub the mixture together until clumps form. Place the bowl in the refrigerator until ready to use.

 3 In a large bowl, with a wooden spoon, gently stir together the apple slices, lemon juice, cinnamon, nutmeg, and cloves. Spoon into a 9- or 10-inch pie plate.

 4 Remove the crumb topping from the refrigerator. Sprinkle the crumbs evenly over the apples in the dish.

5 Bake 40 to 45 minutes or until apples are tender and topping is crisp and lightly browned. Transfer to rack to cool slightly before serving.

What color apple comes next?

ernie's Banana Cream pie in the sky

Preparation time: 30 minutes • Baking time: 23 minutes • Makes 8 servings

Instead of whipped cream, this luscious pie is capped with a soft meringue made with whipped egg whites and confectioner's sugar.

ingredients

Graham Cracker Crust

- 12 whole regular or low-fat honey graham crackers (6 ounces)
- 1 large egg white
- 2 tablespoons olive or vegetable oil

Filling and Topping

- 4 large eggs, separated
- 2 cups low-fat milk
- 1 tablespoon olive oil
- ½ cup granulated sugar
- 2 tablespoons cornstarch
- 1½ teaspoons vanilla extract
- 3 medium bananas, thinly sliced
- ¼ cup confectioner's sugar

equipment

- Pie plate (9-inch)
- Large plastic food storage bag
- Rolling pin
- Fork
- Medium bowls (3)
- Whisk
- Electric mixer
- Medium saucepan
- Whisk for saucepan
- Cooling rack

1 Preheat the oven to 350°F. Lightly grease a 9-inch pie plate.

2 Kids! Place the graham crackers in a large plastic food storage bag. With a rolling pin, gently roll back and forth over the bag to crush the cookies to fine crumbs.

3 Kids! In a medium bowl, use a fork to stir together the one egg white and the oil until blended. Stir in the graham cracker crumbs. Press the mixture evenly across the bottom and up the side of the pie plate.

4 Bake the crust for 8 minutes. Set aside on rack to cool slightly. Leave oven on.

5 Meanwhile, in another medium bowl, whisk together the egg yolks, milk, and oil until smooth. In a medium saucepan, whisk together the granulated sugar and cornstarch. Add the milk mixture to the saucepan and whisk until well-blended.

6 Place the saucepan over medium heat, whisking constantly, for 10 minutes, until mixture comes to a boil and starts to thicken. Remove from heat and whisk in the vanilla. Stir in the bananas. Set aside.

7 In a medium bowl and with an electric mixer and perfectly clean beaters, beat the egg whites at medium speed until foamy. Gradually add confectioner's sugar, beating until glossy, stiff peaks form.

8 Kids! Pour the warm pudding with bananas into the crust. Spoon the egg white topping over the filling, spreading to the edge of the pie to meet the crust and to seal the filling completely.

9 Bake 12 to 15 minutes or until topping is golden brown. Transfer pie to rack to cool completely. Refrigerate until ready to serve.

Tip: In a pinch, you can substitute a store-bought graham cracker or other cookie crumb pie crust for homemade and skip the pre-baking in step 2.

Sometimes when I start saying BANANA, it's hard to stop. Banananananana . . .

85

Rosita's De-Lucious strawberry mango Tart

Preparation time: 20 minutes • Baking time: 1 hour plus 1 hour standing time in oven • Makes 8 servings

This incredible-looking dessert is deceptively easy to make, and the kids can participate at every stage. Only one note: it is normal for a meringue shell to crumble easily, so handle with care while filling and serving.

ingredients

Meringue Shell

- Cooking spray and flour for dusting the baking sheet
- 3 large egg whites, at room temperature
- ¼ teaspoon cream of tartar
- ½ cup sugar
- ¼ teaspoon vanilla

Yogurt-Ricotta Crème Filling

- ½ cup part-skim ricotta cheese
- ½ cup low-fat plain Greek-style yogurt
- ¼ cup sugar
- ¼ teaspoon vanilla extract
- 1 teaspoon grated lemon or orange rind (optional)

Topping

- 1 mango, pared and sliced thinly
- 1 pint strawberries, hulled and sliced
- 1 kiwi, pared, halved, cored, and sliced thinly (optional)

equipment

- Baking sheet
- Aluminum foil
- Cake pan (9-inch diameter)
- Medium bowl
- Electric mixer
- Measuring cups
- Measuring spoons
- Rubber spatula
- Toothpick
- Small bowl

1 Preheat the oven to 300°F. Cover a large baking sheet with foil. Lightly grease the foil. Sprinkle lightly and evenly with flour. Invert a 9-inch diameter cake pan in the center of the baking sheet.

 2 Use your finger to trace a circle in the flour around the edge of the cake pan. Ask an adult to remove the cake pan and set the baking sheet aside.

3 In a medium bowl, with an electric mixer at medium-high speed and perfectly clean beaters, beat the egg whites and cream of tartar until foamy. Add sugar, a little at a time, beating after each addition until sugar dissolves before adding more. Beat until glossy stiff peaks form. Beat in the vanilla. This is called the meringue.

Tip: If you like, you can substitute the graham cracker crust from Ernie's Banana Cream Pie in the Sky (page 84) for the meringue shell in this recipe.

 4 With the help of an adult, spread half the meringue evenly inside the circle you traced on the baking sheet.

5 Spoon the remaining meringue all around the edge of the circle to form the sides of the tart shell. Gently run the back of a spoon around the edge of the meringue to seal the side to the base.

6 Place the meringue shell in the oven and reduce the oven temperature to 250°F. Bake for 1 hour or until the shell is firm and a toothpick inserted in the center comes out clean. Turn the oven off and let the shell dry in the oven for at least 1 hour.

 7 Meanwhile, prepare the filling. In a small bowl, with a rubber spatula, stir together the ricotta cheese, yogurt, sugar, vanilla, and lemon or orange rind, if using. Cover and refrigerate until ready to use.

 8 With the help of an adult, just before serving, gently spread the yogurt filling over the middle of the cooled meringue shell. Arrange the fruit on top. Carefully cut into wedges and transfer to serving plates. (It is normal for the meringue shell to crumble.)

Mangoes grow in warm places—like Mexico, where I was born. Mango trees can live to be hundreds of years old!

cookies and bars

Baking cookies with Mom or Dad—now that's a sweet memory! For many grown-up kids, it's their first food memory. As cookies bake, they fill the kitchen with the unforgettable smells of melting chocolate, sweet spices, and caramelizing sugar. On a practical note, cookie-making teaches all the basic baking skills, such as measuring, mixing, stirring, dropping dough onto baking sheets, and using a rolling pin.

It's simple to cut back on sugar and saturated fats and use ingredients that are rich in vitamins and fiber, such as whole-grain flour, wheat germ, oats, pumpkin, ground nuts, seeds, and dried fruit.

Good nutrition is all about balance. Satisfy your child's sweet tooth (and your own!) with cookies and bars that have been designed to be just a bit healthier but still delicious, fun to eat, and full of memories.

Bert's favorite lemony oat sugar cookies

Preparation time: 20 minutes plus chilling time
Baking time: 10 minutes per batch • Makes about 6 dozen (72) cookies

Lemon rind and juice give these crisp cookies a refreshing citrus flavor.

Tip: Two lemons will provide enough grated rind and juice for these cookies. Grate off just the yellow peel, not the bitter white pith below the peel. To get the most juice from the fruit, roll it gently on the counter under the palm of your hand before cutting.

ingredients

- 2½ cups all-purpose flour
- 2 teaspoons baking powder
- ¼ teaspoon salt
- ½ cup (1 stick) butter
- 2 cups sugar
- 2 large eggs
- ⅓ cup olive oil
- 3 tablespoons lemon juice
- 2 teaspoons finely grated lemon rind
- 1½ cups regular or quick-cooking oats
- Sugar

equipment

- Medium bowl
- Whisk
- Measuring cups
- Measuring spoons
- Large bowl
- Electric mixer
- Wooden spoon
- Teaspoon
- Plastic wrap for wrapping dough
- Small cup
- Baking sheets
- Cooling rack

 1 In a medium bowl, whisk together the flour, baking powder, and salt; set aside.

2 In a large bowl, with an electric mixer, beat the butter and sugar until light and fluffy.

 3 Add the eggs, one at a time, to the butter mixture, beating after each addition. Beat in oil, lemon juice, and lemon rind. With a wooden spoon, stir in flour mixture and oats until well-mixed. Wrap and refrigerate dough until well-chilled, at least 1 hour.

4 Preheat the oven to 375°F. Lightly oil baking sheets.

 5 Use a teaspoon to scoop the dough into 1-inch balls. Place balls, several inches apart, on oiled cookie sheets. Flatten each ball slightly with the bottom of a cup that has been dipped in sugar.

6 Bake cookies 8 to 10 minutes or until lightly browned around the edges. Transfer the baking pan to a rack for 1 minute, then use wide spatula to transfer cookies to a rack to cool completely. Store in airtight container for up to 3 days.

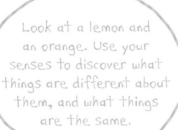

Look at a lemon and an orange. Use your senses to discover what things are different about them, and what things are the same.

cookie monster's cookie·on·a·stick

Preparation time: 25 minutes • Baking time: 35 minutes per batch • Makes 2 dozen (24) cookies

You can bake these like regular cut-out cookies, without the sticks, but on special occasions, it's fun for kids to enjoy "cookie pops." These buttery cookies contain nutrient-rich wheat germ.

ingredients

Cookies

- 1½ cups all-purpose flour
- ½ cup toasted wheat germ
- 1 cup butter, slightly softened
- ½ cup confectioner's sugar
- 1 egg yolk
- ½ teaspoon vanilla extract

Decorating Icing (optional)

- 2 tablespoons pasteurized liquid egg whites
- ¼ teaspoon almond extract
- 1 to 1½ cups confectioner's sugar
- Food coloring (optional)

equipment

- Small bowl
- Whisk
- Measuring cups
- Measuring spoons
- Medium bowls (2)
- Electric mixer
- Rubber spatula
- Rolling pin
- Cookie cutters (2½-inch length or diameter)
- Baking sheets
- Ice pop sticks
- Cooling rack

Tip: For icing, you can use vanilla extract or lemon extract in place of almond.

1 Preheat the oven to 300°F.

2 **Kids!** In a small bowl, whisk together 1 cup of the flour with the wheat germ.

3 In a medium bowl, with an electric mixer on medium-low speed, combine butter and sugar until creamy and well-blended. Beat in the egg yolk and vanilla until blended. Gently fold in the flour mixture (in the mixer or by hand with a rubber spatula), a little at a time, until well-mixed.

4 **Kids!** With the help of an adult, sprinkle the remaining flour on your work surface and lightly knead the dough. Roll the dough out to ¼-inch thickness. Using 2½-inch cookie cutters, cut out cookies. Reroll scraps and repeat. Transfer the cookies to ungreased baking sheets. Carefully insert an ice pop stick halfway up through the bottom of each cookie.

5 Bake the cookies until lightly browned on the bottoms, about 30 to 35 minutes. Transfer the baking sheet to cooling rack. Let cookies cool completely on sheet.

6 If you'd like, prepare the optional decorator icing: In a medium bowl, stir together the egg whites and almond extract until frothy. Gradually stir in confectioner's sugar and food coloring, if using, until smooth and stiff. Spoon icing into a piping bag or plastic food storage bag with a tiny corner snipped off diagonally for piping. Press the bag gently to pipe icing around the edge of each cookie or to create patterns on the cookies.

There are 12 cookies in a dozen.

But "baker's dozen" means 13. Cowabunga! But do not eat stick. Not tasty.

Big Bird's sesame seed Biscuits

Preparation time: 15 minutes • Baking time: 20 minutes • Makes 3 dozen (36) cookies

Big Bird says birdseed never tasted this good! Adults and kids will keep coming back for more of these crunchy-sweet cookies.

Tip: You can usually buy sesame seeds in the spice aisle or in bulk packaging at health stores and larger supermarkets.

ingredients

- 1 cup sesame seeds
- 1½ cups all-purpose flour
- ½ cup whole-wheat flour
- ¾ cup granulated sugar
- 1 teaspoon baking powder
- ¼ teaspoon salt
- 1 large egg
- ¼ cup (½ stick) butter, softened
- ¼ cup olive oil
- 2 tablespoons water
- ½ teaspoon vanilla extract

equipment

- Large heavy skillet
- Large bowl
- Whisk
- Measuring cups
- Measuring spoons
- Electric mixer
- Rubber spatula
- Tablespoon
- Baking sheets
- Cooling racks

1 Preheat the oven to 350°F. In a large heavy skillet over medium heat, toast sesame seeds for 2 to 3 minutes, or until they just turn light golden brown, shaking skillet and stirring frequently to keep them moving. Remove the seeds from the skillet and set aside.

2 In a large bowl, whisk together the all-purpose flour, whole-wheat flour, sugar, baking powder, and salt.

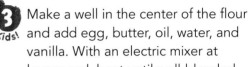 **3** Make a well in the center of the flour and add egg, butter, oil, water, and vanilla. With an electric mixer at low speed, beat until well-blended, occasionally scraping bowl with a rubber spatula. Stir in ½ cup of the toasted seeds.

4 Use a tablespoon to scoop the dough and shape into 1½-inch logs.

5 Roll logs in remaining toasted sesame seeds. Place about 1 inch apart on ungreased baking sheets.

6 Bake 20 minutes, or until firm to the touch. Transfer the baking sheets to racks to cool slightly. Store in airtight container for up to 1 week.

Sesame seeds grow inside pods on flowering sesame plants.

Tip: Snickerdoodles store well and mail well. To mail cookies, wrap them in plastic wrap or aluminum foil several times, then pack them tightly in a small, sturdy box. Place that box in a larger box with plenty of cushioning material. It is best to choose overnight delivery when mailing fresh food.

ernie's All-American snickerdoodles

Preparation time: 15 minutes • Baking time: 12 minutes per batch • Makes about 5 dozen (60) cookies

Are these the same snickerdoodles your grandmother used to make? No, not quite. Half the butter is replaced with healthier olive oil, we've cut the sugar just a little, and there's wheat germ for extra goodness. Are these snickerdoodles just as cinnamony good? You bet they are!

ingredients

- **3 cups all-purpose flour**
- **½ cup wheat germ**
- **1 tablespoon baking powder**
- **1 teaspoon baking soda**
- **¼ teaspoon salt**
- **¼ teaspoon ground cinnamon**
- **½ cup (1 stick) butter**
- **1¾ cups sugar**
- **2 large eggs**
- **½ cup olive oil**
- **1 tablespoon vanilla extract**
- **¼ cup sugar mixed with ½ teaspoon ground cinnamon**

equipment

- **Medium bowl**
- **Whisk**
- **Measuring cups**
- **Measuring spoons**
- **Large bowl**
- **Electric mixer**
- **Teaspoon**
- **Baking sheets**
- **Cooling racks**

1 Preheat the oven to 375°F.

2 In a medium bowl, whisk together the flour, wheat germ, baking powder, baking soda, salt, and cinnamon.

3 Kids! In a large bowl, with the help of an adult and with an electric mixer on medium speed, cream the butter. Add the sugar and beat until blended. Add the eggs, oil, and vanilla and mix thoroughly. Add the dry ingredients and mix just until blended.

4 Use a teaspoon to scoop the dough into 1-inch balls.

5 Kids! Roll the dough balls in the sugar-cinnamon mixture to coat. Place on ungreased baking sheets, 2½ inches apart.

6 Bake 10 to 12 minutes or until the surface is puffed, golden, and slightly cracked. Transfer the baking sheets to cool for 2 minutes, then transfer cookies to rack to cool completely.

"Snickerdoodles" is a funny word. Say it three times fast. Then think of some other silly-sounding words!

Tip: You can substitute other finely ground nuts, such as pecans, walnuts, or hazelnuts, for the almonds.

Rosita's Lovely Little Almond Tea Cakes

Preparation time: 20 minutes • Baking time: 12 minutes per batch • Makes about 3 dozen (36) cookies

These cookies remind Rosita of the melt-in-your mouth, Mexican cookies her mom makes for festive occasions. Elmo says they remind him of snowballs!

Ingredients

- 1¾ cups all-purpose flour
- ½ cup whole-wheat flour
- ¼ cup plus 1½ cups confectioner's sugar
- 3 tablespoons cornstarch
- ⅛ teaspoon salt
- ¾ cup olive oil or vegetable oil
- 1 teaspoon vanilla extract
- ¾ cup almonds, ground

Equipment

- Large bowl
- Whisk
- Measuring cups
- Measuring spoons
- Rubber spatula
- Teaspoon
- Baking sheets
- Cooling racks
- Medium bowl

1 Preheat the oven to 400°F.

2 Kids! In a large bowl, whisk together the all-purpose flour, whole-wheat flour, ¼ cup confectioner's sugar, cornstarch, and salt until well-mixed.

3 Kids! With a rubber spatula, gradually stir the oil into the flour mixture until well-mixed. Stir in the vanilla and almonds.

4 Kids! Use a teaspoon to scoop the dough into 1-inch balls. Place balls 1 inch apart on ungreased cookie sheets.

5 Bake the cookies until just set, 10 to 12 minutes, being careful not to let them overcook. Cool cookies on the baking sheet on a rack for 2 minutes, before transferring cookies to the rack to cool slightly. Pour the remaining 1½ cups confectioner's sugar into a medium bowl.

6 Kids! While the cookies are still warm but cool enough to handle, roll them in a bowl of confectioner's sugar. Place them back on the rack to cool completely. Then roll the cookies in confectioner's sugar again.

¡Deliciosa!

Oscar's Gooey, Chewy PBJ Cookies

Preparation time: 20 minutes • Baking time: 10 minutes per batch
Makes 5 dozen (60) individual cookies or 2½ dozen (30) sandwich cookies

Sandwich these drop cookies together with a little jam, or skip the jam and enjoy the cookies on their own with a tall glass of cold milk.

ingredients

- ¾ cup all-purpose flour
- ½ teaspoon salt
- ½ teaspoon baking soda
- ¼ teaspoon baking powder
- 1 cup uncooked, quick-cooking oats
- ¼ cup butter, softened
- ½ cup creamy peanut butter
- ½ cup granulated sugar
- ½ cup packed light brown sugar
- 1 large egg
- ¼ cup olive oil
- 1 teaspoon vanilla extract
- ½ cup jam or fruit-spread (optional)

equipment

- **Baking sheets**
- **Medium bowl**
- **Whisk**
- **Measuring cups**
- **Measuring spoons**
- **Large bowl**
- **Electric mixer**
- **Wooden spoon**
- **Teaspoon**
- **Plastic fork**
- **Cooling rack**

1 Preheat the oven to 350°F. Lightly grease baking sheets.

 2 In a medium bowl, whisk together the flour, salt, baking soda, and baking powder until well-mixed. Stir in oats.

 3 In a large bowl, with electric mixer at medium-low speed, combine the butter, peanut butter, granulated sugar, and brown sugar until creamy and well-blended. Beat in the egg, oil, and vanilla just until blended. With the mixer or by hand with a wooden spoon, stir in the flour mixture until well-mixed.

 4 Drop dough by teaspoonfuls onto oiled baking sheets. Use a plastic fork to press gently on cookie dough and flatten to ¼-inch thick rounds.

5 Bake 10 minutes or until cookies are lightly browned. Cool cookies on the baking sheet on a rack for 2 minutes, then transfer cookies to the rack to cool completely.

 6 To make sandwich cookies, spread half the cookies each with a scant ½ teaspoon jam, then top with remaining cookies.

> **Tip:** You can store the single cookies in a covered container at room temperature for up to a few days and sandwich them together just before serving. Once they are sandwiched together, the cookies will hold up best in a covered container in the refrigerator.

What lives in the ocean, has tentacles, and sticks to the roof of your mouth? A peanut butter and jellyfish! Heh heh heh!

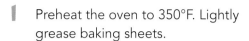

cowboy elmo's
Best Brownies in the west

Preparation time: 15 minutes • Baking time: 25 minutes • Makes 2 dozen (24) brownies

Chocolate chips make these fudgy brownies yummy for those extra-special occasions, while some whole-wheat flour and olive oil add some nutrition.

ingredients

- 1 cup all-purpose flour
- ⅓ cup whole-wheat flour
- ¾ cup unsweetened cocoa powder
- ½ teaspoon baking powder
- ¼ teaspoon salt
- 1¾ cups sugar
- ½ cup olive oil or vegetable oil
- ¼ cup (½ stick) butter, melted
- 3 tablespoons low-fat milk
- 2 large eggs
- 1 teaspoon vanilla extract
- ½ cup chocolate chips

equipment

- Baking pan (13×9×2-inch)
- Aluminum foil for lining pan
- Medium bowl
- Whisk
- Measuring cups
- Measuring spoons
- Large bowl
- Wooden spoon
- Rubber spatula
- Toothpick
- Cooling rack

1 Preheat the oven to 350°F. Line a 13x9x2-inch baking pan with aluminum foil. Lightly grease the foil.

2 In a medium bowl, whisk together the all-purpose flour, whole-wheat flour, cocoa powder, baking powder, and salt.

3 In a large bowl, stir together the sugar, oil, butter, and milk. Stir in the eggs and vanilla until well-blended. Gradually stir in the flour mixture until blended.

4 Add the chocolate chips. Use a wooden spoon to stir the chips into the dough.

5 Use a rubber spatula to spread the batter evenly in the pan.

6 Bake 20 to 25 minutes, or until a toothpick inserted in the center comes out clean. Transfer the baking pan to a rack to cool completely. Lift from the pan by the foil and cut into 24 brownies.

> Ask a grown-up to cut 24 brownies in all, in 4 long rows. How many brownies do you count in each row?

Tip: You can substitute cinnamon chips, white chocolate chips, or regular chocolate chips for the butterscotch in these bars.

Abby's Best-ever Pumpkin Bars with Butterscotch Chips

Preparation time: 20 minutes • Baking time: 40 minutes • Makes 2 dozen (24) bars

These cake-like bar cookies are a great make-ahead treat because they last for days and days.

Ingredients

- 2 cups all-purpose flour
- ¼ cup toasted wheat germ
- 1 tablespoon pumpkin pie spice mix
- 1 teaspoon baking soda
- ½ teaspoon salt
- ½ cup (1 stick) butter, softened
- 1 cup sugar
- 1 large egg
- 1 cup canned pumpkin puree
- ½ cup olive or vegetable oil
- 1 tablespoon vanilla extract
- 1 cup butterscotch chips

Equipment

- Baking pan (13×9-inch)
- Medium bowl
- Whisk or fork
- Large bowl
- Electric mixer
- Wooden spoon
- Toothpick
- Cooling rack

1 Preheat the oven to 350°F. Lightly oil and flour a 13x9-inch baking pan.

 2 In a medium bowl, whisk together the flour, wheat germ, spice mix, baking soda, and salt.

 3 In a large bowl, with an electric mixer on medium speed, cream the butter and sugar. Beat in the egg, pumpkin, oil, and vanilla. On low speed, beat in the flour mixture just until blended.

 4 Use a wooden spoon to stir in the butterscotch chips.

5 Spread the batter evenly in the prepared pan.

6 Bake until a toothpick inserted in the center comes out clean, about 35 minutes. Transfer the baking pan to a rack to cool completely. When cool, cut into 24 bars.

Chip chip hooray!

celebration cupcakes and cakes

For most families, the secret to keeping sweets to a minimum is not to restrict them completely, but to teach children from early on that rich desserts are "sometimes foods," reserved for special occasions. A special cake or cupcake is often a big part of birthdays, holidays, or family celebrations. It is a tradition that children look forward to with great anticipation.

You can minimize fat and sugar in dessert recipes, but remember that these ingredients are often necessary to create rich flavor and to ensure the "kitchen chemistry" essential for baking success. Try using healthier fats, such as olive oil or vegetable oil, whenever possible, for some or all of the saturated fat found in butter.

Accustom children to smaller serving sizes of richer foods, and help them develop a taste for desserts with whole-grains, yogurt, fruits, and other wholesome ingredients. Top cupcakes and cakes with just a dollop of frosting or a dusting of confectioner's sugar—a little goes a long way.

Oscar's Applicious Cupcakes

Preparation time: 20 minutes • Baking time: 20 minutes • Makes 24 cupcakes

Apples, applesauce, a little whole-wheat flour, and a maple-flavored yogurt and cream cheese frosting make this cupcake about as wholesome as a sweet treat can be. If you leave off the frosting, these cupcakes could double as fruity muffins for breakfast.

Tips:

• Spoon the frosting into a decorating bag fitted with a wide tip and let the kids help squeeze just a small swirl of frosting on each cupcake.

• Alternatively, show them how to use two spoons, one for scooping and one for pushing the scooped frosting off the other spoon, to place a small dollop of frosting on each cupcake.

Ingredients

Cupcakes

- 1½ cups all-purpose flour
- 1 cup whole-wheat flour
- 1½ cups sugar
- 1 teaspoon baking powder
- 1 teaspoon baking soda
- 1½ teaspoons cinnamon
- ½ teaspoon freshly grated nutmeg
- ½ teaspoon salt
- 2 large eggs
- 1½ cups applesauce
- ½ cup olive oil
- 1 cup finely chopped, peeled apple

Maple Frosting

- 4 ounces reduced-fat cream cheese
- ¼ cup low-fat plain Greek-style yogurt
- ⅓ cup packed light brown sugar
- ¼ cup real maple syrup
- Apple slices, if desired

Equipment

- Muffin pans (24 cups)
- Cupcake liners
- Large bowl
- Whisk
- Measuring cups
- Measuring spoons
- Electric mixer
- Wooden spoon
- Toothpick
- Cooling rack
- Small bowl
- Fork for stirring

Save the apple cores for me!

1 Preheat the oven to 350°F.

2 Line 24 muffin-pan cups with cupcake liners.

3 In a large bowl, whisk all-purpose flour, whole-wheat flour, sugar, baking powder, baking soda, cinnamon, nutmeg, and salt. With mixer at medium-low speed, add the eggs, applesauce, and oil. Mix for 2 to 3 minutes or until well-blended. With a wooden spoon, stir in chopped apples.

4 Use a ¼-cup measuring cup to fill the cupcake liners half-full with batter.

5 Bake 18 to 20 minutes, or until a toothpick inserted into the center comes out clean. Remove the cupcakes from the pan and cool completely on a rack.

6 In a small bowl, use a fork to mash and then stir together the cream cheese, yogurt, brown sugar, and maple syrup until smooth. Refrigerate until cupcakes are cool enough to frost. Top the center of each cupcake with a small dollop of frosting.

7 Decorate, if you like, with a slice of apple.

elmo's Red velvet cupcakes

Preparation time: 20 minutes • Baking time: 20 minutes • Makes 36 cupcakes

These are Elmo's favorite cupcakes because the batter turns slightly red, like him! Your children will love stirring the hot pink beet puree into the yogurt mixture and then mixing it into the batter.

ingredients

Cake

- 2½ cups all-purpose flour
- ½ cup unsweetened cocoa powder
- 1 teaspoon baking powder
- 1 teaspoon baking soda
- ¼ teaspoon salt
- 1 cup low-fat plain yogurt
- 1 can (15 ounces) sliced, no-salt-added beets, drained and pureed with ¼ cup of their liquid until almost smooth
- ½ cup olive oil or vegetable oil
- 1 teaspoon vanilla extract
- ½ cup (1 stick) butter, at room temperature
- 2 cups granulated sugar
- 5 large eggs

Whipped Cream Topping

- ½ pint heavy or whipping cream
- ¼ cup confectioner's sugar

equipment

- Muffin pans
- Cupcake liners
- Large bowls (2)
- Whisk
- Measuring cups
- Measuring spoons
- Electric mixer
- Medium bowl
- Rubber spatula
- Toothpick
- Cooling rack

1 Preheat the oven to 325°F.

 2 Kids! Line 36 muffin pan cups with cupcake liners.

3 Kids! In a large bowl, whisk together the flour, cocoa powder, baking powder, baking soda, and salt. In a medium bowl, with a rubber spatula, stir together the yogurt, beet puree, oil, and vanilla until smooth.

4 Kids! In another large bowl, with an electric mixer at medium-high speed, cream the butter and granulated sugar until fluffy. Add the eggs, one at a time, beating well after each. Add the flour mixture alternately with the yogurt mixture.

Tip: In place of whipped cream, you can use the vanilla buttercream frosting from Zoe's Share-with-the-Class Sweet Vanilla Babycakes (page 112), or simply sprinkle these cupcakes with confectioner's sugar or cocoa powder from a mesh sieve.

 5 Kids! Use a ¼-cup dry measure to fill the cupcake liners half-full with batter.

6 Bake for 18 to 20 minutes or until a toothpick inserted in the center of a cupcake comes out clean. Transfer pans to racks to cool for 10 minutes. Transfer cupcakes from pans to rack to cool completely before frosting.

7 Shortly before serving, in a medium bowl with an electric mixer on medium-high speed, beat the heavy cream and confectioner's sugar until stiff peaks just form.

8 Kids! Use a spoon to put a small dollop of whipped cream topping on each cupcake just before serving.

For yummy vegetables, you can't beat beets! Hee hee!

ZOE'S SHARE·WITH·THE·CLASS SWEET VANILLA BABYCAKES

Preparation time: 25 minutes • Baking time: 60 minutes • Makes 12 servings

A mini muffin pan makes light little cakes that are the perfect size for a special classroom celebration. Frost with just a dab of buttercream, and top with fresh raspberries or blueberries, or a few mini chocolate chips or sprinkles.

Ingredients

Cake

- 1 cup all-purpose flour
- 2 tablespoons toasted wheat germ
- 1 teaspoon baking powder
- Pinch salt
- 4 large eggs, separated
- ⅔ cup sugar
- ¼ cup low-fat (1%) milk
- 2 tablespoons olive oil or vegetable oil
- 1 teaspoon vanilla extract

Vanilla Buttercream Frosting

- 1 cup confectioner's sugar
- 2 tablespoons butter, softened
- 2 teaspoons low-fat (1%) milk
- ¼ teaspoon vanilla

Equipment

- Mini muffin pans
- Mini paper muffin pan liners (48)
- Measuring cups
- Measuring spoons
- Large bowl
- Whisk
- Fork
- Medium bowls (2)
- Electric mixer
- Rubber spatula
- Toothpick
- Cooling racks

1   Preheat the oven to 350°F.

 2   Line 48 mini muffin cups with mini paper liners.

 3   In a large bowl, whisk together the flour, wheat germ, baking powder, and salt. In a medium bowl, stir together the egg yolks, ⅓ cup of the sugar, the milk, oil, and vanilla until well-blended. Use a fork to stir the yolk mixture into the flour mixture until well-mixed.

4   In a medium bowl, with an electric mixer on medium-high speed and clean beaters, beat the egg whites with the remaining ⅓ cup sugar until soft peaks form.

5   With a rubber spatula, fold a cupful of the beaten whites into the batter to lighten. Gently fold in the remaining whites just until incorporated. Use a measuring tablepoon to spoon the batter into the lined muffin cups, filling each one-half to three-quarters full. If you are baking in batches, refrigerate the batter between batches.

6   Bake for 8 to 10 minutes or until a toothpick inserted in the center of one cupcake comes out clean. Transfer to racks to cool completely before frosting and serving.

 7   To make frosting, stir together the confectioner's sugar, butter, milk, and vanilla in a medium bowl until smooth. Cover and refrigerate until ready to use. Top each cupcake with just a small dab of frosting.

Tips:

• This recipe makes only a small amount of frosting that is best divided by piping just a dollop in the center of each mini cupcake. If you don't have a decorating bag, spoon the frosting into a zippered plastic food storage bag. Squeeze the frosting down to one corner of the bag and snip off just the tip of that corner with scissors to make a small opening.

• To decorate, top each dollop of frosting with a small raspberry or a few mini chocolate chips.

Which babycake is not like the others?

Big Bird's orange chiffon cake

Preparation time: 20 minutes • Baking time: 1 hour • Makes 12 servings

This big, soft, citrus-y cake is perfect for a special spring celebration.

ingredients

Cake

- **2 cups all-purpose flour or 2¼ cups cake flour**
- **1½ cups granulated sugar**
- **1 tablespoon baking powder**
- **½ teaspoon salt**
- **6 large egg yolks**
- **8 large egg whites**
- **¾ cup orange juice**
- **½ cup olive or vegetable oil**
- **2 tablespoons grated orange rind**
- **2 teaspoons vanilla extract**
- **1 teaspoon cream of tartar**

Citrus Glaze

- **1½ cups confectioner's sugar**
- **2 tablespoons orange juice**
- **1 tablespoon lemon juice**
- **1 teaspoon grated orange rind**

equipment

- **Large bowls (2)**
- **Medium bowl**
- **Whisk**
- **Rubber spatulas (2)**
- **Measuring cups**
- **Measuring spoons**
- **Electric mixer**
- **Wooden spoon**
- **Tube cake pan (10-inch diameter)**
- **Toothpick**
- **Cooling rack**
- **Thin metal spatula or knife**
- **Small bowl**
- **Waxed paper**
- **Large spoon**

1 Preheat the oven to 325°F.

2 In a large bowl, whisk together the flour, ¾ cup of the granulated sugar, baking powder, and salt until well-mixed. In a medium bowl, with a rubber spatula, stir together the egg yolks, orange juice, oil, orange rind, and vanilla. Make a well in the center of the flour mixture, add the yolk mixture, and whisk together until the batter is smooth.

3 In another large bowl, with an electric mixer at medium speed and clean beaters, beat the egg whites until foamy. Add the cream of tartar and beat until stiff peaks form. Beat in the rest of the granulated sugar, a little at a time, beating well after each addition.

 4 Use a wooden spoon to stir one-third of the egg whites into the batter until well-mixed.

5 Gently fold in the remaining whites just until completely blended. With a spatula, scrape the batter into an ungreased 10-inch diameter deep tube pan.

6 Bake for 1 hour or until a toothpick inserted into the cake comes out clean. Turn the pan upside down onto a cooling rack or heatproof counter. Let the cake cool completely in the pan. When cool, run a long thin spatula or knife around the outer and inner edge of the pan. Turn the cake out onto the rack.

 7 Meanwhile, in a small bowl, stir together the confectioner's sugar, orange juice, lemon juice, and orange rind until well-mixed. Place a piece of waxed paper under the rack. Spoon the glaze over the top of the cake and let it drip down the sides. (You can scrape the excess glaze from the waxed paper with a knife or spoon, thin it out with a little orange juice if necessary, and pour it back over the cake.)

Tips:
- If you are buying a new tube pan, choose one with feet and a removable bottom to make cooling and removing the cake from the pan easier.

- To dress this cake up for special occasions, decorate the top and around the base with clusters of fresh raspberries and mint leaves.

Oranges are citrus fruits, like lemons, limes, and grapefruits. Very refreshing!

Cookie Monster's Pineapple Carrot Birthday Cake

Preparation time: 25 minutes • Baking time: 40 minutes • Makes 12 to 16 servings

ingredients

Cake

- 2 cups all-purpose flour
- 1 cup sugar
- 1 teaspoon baking powder
- 1 teaspoon baking soda
- ¾ teaspoon salt
- 1 teaspoon cinnamon
- ½ teaspoon nutmeg
- 4 large eggs
- ½ cup olive oil
- ¾ cup low-fat plain yogurt
- 2 teaspoons vanilla extract
- 3 large carrots, peeled and grated (2 cups)
- 1 cup drained, crushed pineapple packed in juice
- ½ cup golden or dark seedless raisins

Cream Cheese–Yogurt Frosting

- 1 package (8 ounces) reduced-fat cream cheese, at room temperature
- 1 cup low-fat plain Greek-style yogurt
- ½ cup sugar
- 2 teaspoons grated lemon rind (optional)

equipment

- 2 cake pans (9×2-inch)
- Waxed paper
- Medium bowls (2)
- Whisks (2)
- Measuring cups
- Measuring spoons
- Large bowl
- Wooden spoon
- Toothpick
- Cooling racks
- Serving plate

A celebration cake doesn't get much healthier than this one! Even the traditionally heavy cream cheese frosting is lightened up with sweetened Greek-style yogurt.

1 Preheat the oven to 350°F. Lightly grease two 9x2-inch cake pans. Line the pans with waxed paper, and grease and flour the paper. Tap out any excess flour.

2 Kids! In a medium bowl, whisk together the flour, sugar, baking powder, baking soda, salt, cinnamon, and nutmeg.

3 Kids! In a large bowl, whisk together the eggs, oil, yogurt, and vanilla until well-mixed. With a wooden spoon, gradually add the flour mixture to the oil mixture and stir until blended. Stir in the carrots, pineapple, and raisins, if using.

4 Divide the batter evenly between the prepared pans.

5 Bake 40 minutes or until a toothpick inserted into the center of the cakes comes out clean. Cool cakes in pans on racks for 20 minutes. Turn out onto racks, peel off waxed paper, and cool completely before frosting.

Tip: You can make and frost this cake the day before using. Store, covered, in the refrigerator and bring to room temperature 30 minutes before slicing and serving.

6 Kids! Meanwhile, make the frosting: In another medium bowl, stir together the cream cheese, yogurt, sugar, and lemon rind, if using. Refrigerate at least 1 hour before frosting the cake.

7 Kids! To frost the cake, place one layer on a plate. Use a plastic knife to spread ½ cup of the frosting over the top of the cake. Top with second layer of cake. Use the remaining frosting to cover the top and sides of the cake.

Many pineapples grow in Hawaii. Aloha, baby!

grover's Red, white, & Blue celebration cake

Preparation time: 20 minutes • Baking time: 30 minutes • Makes 1 sheet cake (12 to 16 servings)

Ingredients

Cake

- 3 cups all-purpose flour

- 1 tablespoon baking powder

- 1 teaspoon baking soda

- ½ teaspoon salt

- 1½ cups low-fat lemon-flavored yogurt

- 1½ teaspoons vanilla extract

- 1 cup (2 sticks) unsalted butter, softened

- 1¾ cups granulated sugar

- 4 large eggs

Lemon Buttercream Frosting

- ¼ cup (½ stick) butter, softened

- 1 tablespoon fresh lemon juice

- 1 teaspoon grated lemon rind

- 1¼ cups confectioner's sugar

- 2 tablespoons low-fat milk or water

Fruit Topping

- ½ pint fresh blueberries

- 1 pint fresh raspberries or cut-up strawberries

equipment

- Baking pan (13×9×2-inch)

- Medium bowl

- Whisk

- Rubber spatula

- Measuring cups

- Measuring spoons

- Small bowls (2)

- Large bowl

- Electric mixer

- Rubber spatula

- Toothpick

- Cooling rack

- Plastic knife

For a Fourth of July celebration, arrange the berries in an American flag design. For other occasions, simply scatter the berries over the top. A thin layer of lemony buttercream frosting "glues" the berries to the cake.

1　Preheat the oven to 350°F. Lightly grease and flour a 13x9x2-inch baking pan. Shake out any excess flour.

2 Kids! In a medium bowl, whisk together the flour, baking powder, baking soda, and salt. Set aside. In a small bowl, with a rubber spatula, stir together the yogurt and vanilla. Set aside.

3　In a large bowl, with an electric mixer on medium-high, beat the butter and granulated sugar until light and fluffy. Beat in the eggs, one at a time. With the beater on low speed, beat in the flour mixture alternately with the yogurt mixture, beginning and ending with the flour.

4　Scrape the batter evenly into the prepared pan, smoothing the top with a rubber spatula.

5　Bake for 30 minutes or until a toothpick inserted in the center comes out clean. Transfer the pan to a rack to cool completely.

6 Kids! Meanwhile, make the frosting. In a small bowl, with the help of an adult and with an electric mixer on high speed, cream the butter until it is light and fluffy. Beat in the lemon juice and lemon rind. Reduce the speed to low and add the confectioner's sugar, ¼ cup at a time, until well-mixed. Beat in the milk until fully blended.

7 Kids! Use a plastic knife to spread the frosting in a thin layer on the top of the cake. Top with blueberries and raspberries. Refrigerate for up to 2 hours before serving.

Tips:
• Rinse and drain the berries well on paper towels to soak up all excess moisture before placing them on the cake.

• Just for fun, have the kids gently stir 1½ cups of mixed berries into the cake batter before spreading it in the pan. That way the cake will have berries on the inside and the outside!

Cute little berries start with the letter B. What else can you think of that starts with B? Bravo! You are beautiful and brainy.

ernie's halloween marble cake

Preparation time: 25 minutes • Baking time: 60 minutes • Makes 12 servings

This is the perfect cake to bake for Halloween or any fall or winter occasion— or to surprise Dad on Father's Day.

Tip: In a pinch, you can substitute drained canned yams or canned pumpkin for the squash or sweet potatoes. You can also substitute 2 teaspoons pumpkin pie spice for the cinnamon, ginger, and nutmeg called for in this recipe.

Ingredients

- 3 cups all-purpose flour
- 1¼ cups sugar
- 2 teaspoons baking powder
- 2 teaspoons baking soda
- 1 teaspoon ground cinnamon
- ½ teaspoon ground ginger
- ¼ teaspoon ground nutmeg
- 1 teaspoon salt
- 2 cups cooked winter squash, such as butternut or acorn, or cooked sweet potatoes, scraped from skins
- 1½ cups olive oil
- 4 eggs
- 1½ teaspoons vanilla extract
- 6 ounces semisweet chocolate, melted

Equipment

- Bundt or tube pan (10-inch)
- Medium bowl
- Small bowls (2)
- Measuring cups
- Measuring spoons
- Whisk
- Large bowl
- Electric mixer
- Spoon
- Large spoons
- Plastic knife
- Toothpick
- Cooling rack

1 Preheat the oven to 350°F. Lightly grease a 10-inch Bundt or tube pan. Dust the pan completely with flour.

2 In a medium bowl, whisk together flour, sugar, baking powder, baking soda, cinnamon, ginger, nutmeg, and salt. In a small bowl, use a spoon to mash the squash.

3 With the help of an adult, in a large bowl with electric mixer at medium speed, beat together the squash, olive oil, eggs, and vanilla until very smooth. Beat in the flour mixture until smooth. Transfer one-third of the batter to another small bowl.

4 Carefully stir the melted chocolate into the small bowl of batter.

5 Using large spoons, spoon the batters alternately into the pan. With a plastic knife, swirl together the squash batter and the chocolate batter to get a marbled effect.

6 Bake 50 to 60 minutes or until a toothpick inserted in the center comes out clean and the cake shrinks from the side of the pan. Transfer the pan to a cooling rack for 10 minutes. Turn the cake out onto the rack to cool completely.

> Trick and treat! Can your family and friends guess the tricky, secret veggie ingredient?

Abby Cadabby's Angel Cake

Preparation time: 10 minutes • Baking time: 35 minutes • Makes 12 servings

An angel food cake contains no fat, and this one uses a little less sugar than usual. It's a great base for fresh fruit and berries. Top it with a dollop of whipped cream on special occasions. Fairy delicious!

Ingredients

Cake

- 10 large egg whites (1¼ cups)
- 1 teaspoon cream of tartar
- ¼ teaspoon salt
- 1 cup sugar
- 1 teaspoon vanilla extract
- 1 cup cake flour

Topping

- Chopped fresh fruit or mixed berries
- Whipped cream (optional)

Equipment

- Large bowl
- Electric beater
- Measuring cups
- Measuring spoons
- Rubber spatula
- Angel food tube pan (9-inch diameter)
- Toothpick
- Cooling rack
- Thin metal spatula
- Medium bowl
- Large spoon

Tip: If your angel cake pan has "feet," turn the pan upside down onto a rack or counter and let cool completely, about 2 hours. If it does not have feet, invert the pan over the neck of a filled bottle with a protruding top that fits in the center opening of the pan.

122

1. Set an oven rack to the lowest position, removing other racks, if necessary. Preheat the oven to 350°F.

2. In a large bowl with an electric mixer, beat the egg whites until frothy. Add cream of tartar and salt. Beat until soft peaks form when the mixer is turned off and beater is lifted. (Soft peaks fold over rather than standing up stiff.)

3. Gradually beat in the sugar, then the vanilla, beating after each addition until blended.

4. **Kids!** Add the flour, ¼ cup at a time. With the help of an adult, use a rubber spatula to very gently fold in each addition, just until mixed.

5. Turn the batter into an ungreased, 9-inch-diameter angel food tube pan.

6. Bake until a toothpick inserted in center comes out clean, about 35 minutes. Turn the cake upside down on a cooling rack or heatproof counter until cooled completely. Run a thin metal spatula or knife around the outer edge and inner tube to loosen the cake from the pan. Gently ease the cake out of the pan.

7. To serve, slice the cake with a serrated knife.

8. **Kids!** Just before serving, combine the chopped fruit or berries in a medium bowl. Spoon the fruit over the cake. Top with a dollop of whipped cream, if you like.

It is I, Count von Count, with the number of the day: 10! Ten eggs, count them, ah ah ah! Now count all the fingers on your hands! Ten again! 10 is terrific!

Decorating Tips

most cakes and cookies can get away with just a little frosting, and some don't need any at all. These decorating tips will give you ideas about how to jazz up the sweet stuff without adding a lot of excess sugar and fat.

- Use paper doilies or stencils to create patterns on plain cakes and cupcakes. Place the template over the cake and dust with confectioner's sugar sprinkled through a fine mesh sieve or with a flour sifter. Carefully lift off the template. On dark cakes, use confectioner's sugar alone; on lighter color cakes, mix a little unsweetened cocoa powder with the sugar before sifting.

- Instead of spreading frosting over the entire surface of a cupcake or cake, use a pastry or decorating bag fitted with a star tip or small open tip to pipe a tiny rosette or swirl of icing in the centers of cupcakes or just around the edge of a cake. Place a fresh berry, a thin slice of fruit, or a teddy bear graham cracker in the center of each dollop of frosting.

- If you don't have a pastry or decorating bag for frosting, use a small or medium-size zippered food storage bag. Clip one corner to make a small opening and fill the bag with frosting. The size of the opening will determine the thickness of the frosting. For outlining cookies, snip off a very small corner. For larger dollops of frosting on cupcakes and cakes, snip off about ¼ inch from the corner.

- Use non-edible decorations for cakes. Small, clean, age-appropriate plastic toys and figurines (with no breakable or chokeable parts) will please a child just as much as a sweet frosting. Fancy candles, small paper parasols, and non-poisonous, real flowers are also options for non-edible decorations.

- Decorate the plate. From underneath, tape colorful balloons or garlands around the outer edge of a platter that will hold a cake or cupcakes.

- When frosting the entire surface of a cake or cupcake, use just a thin layer as "glue" to hold pieces of fresh fruit or berries in rows or in a decorative pattern.

- Melt semi-sweet or white chocolate chips in a small cup in the microwave oven at half power or on the stovetop in a small double-boiler, stirring often. If using a microwave oven, check and stir every 45 seconds. Dip a spoon into the fully melted chocolate and drizzle it from the tip in a zigzag pattern over cookies, bars, cupcakes, or cakes.

About the Authors

Susan McQuillan is a nutritionist and food writer who has written extensively about healthy eating. She has contributed many articles and recipes to magazines such as *Woman's Day, Family Circle, American Health, Prevention,* and *Cooking Light.* Susan has a lot in common with Cookie Monster; she loves to eat healthy foods like fruits and vegetables, but she also loves cookies! Susan would like to thank Elmo and the rest of the Sesame Street gang for teaching her daughter Molly all about the ABCs and 1-2-3s, and for all the bright ideas they inspired for this cookbook.

Leslie Kimmelman is an editor at Sesame Workshop and the author of many books for young children.

Thanks
to the contributing chefs and recipe tasters!

Index

How many Twiddlebugs did you count? (Don't count me.) There are 27!